Jesus' first invitation was to make us fishers of men, and His last command was for us to make disciples. It may very well be that making disciples is the last thing many churches are interested in. This book matters because the time for cheap Jesus subscribers is over, and the time for the slow work of incarnation has come. Read this book!

—**Nathan Finochio,** *Co-founder of TheosU*

James is a gift to the Body of Christ. His wisdom and joy has impacted countless people over the past two decades and his love for Jesus and His Church only grows. I'm so grateful for this prophetic challenge to re-engage in the great command of the King, "make disciples". James has committed his life to this call and my life and ministry has been deeply impacted because of it.

—**Dan Lian,** *Teaching Pastor NewSpring Church South Carolina, USA*

Discipleship is a way of life every follower of Christ is called to live. James Murray not only lives this out but has a unique and very practical way in unpacking the realities of discipleship that will not only help you gain understanding but give you tools to be an effective disciple and discipler of people.

—**Luke Dejong,** *Senior Pastor, LIFE Church*

James is a brilliant minded, people focused, Christ centred leader. His real world approach, biblical insight and practical help will guide any leader or follower of Jesus to take their next steps & see greater fruit in their discipleship journey.

—**Josh Greenwood,** *Lead Pastor, Futures Church, Adelaide*

This book is for the serious Kingdom builders among us. Given that discipleship in church serves as the bricks and mortar for building God's Kingdom, this book is a must read. It serves as a blueprint for conforming people to the likeness of Christ. For churches wanting to dial up their discipline, join James Murray as he takes you on an faith-filled journey of practical discipleship. You are invited.

—**Dr Robi, Sonderegger,** *(Clinical Psychologist), Peoplecare Global GmbH*

James Murray has written a much needed book for followers of Christ. Discipleship is a word thrown around but not often clearly defined or unpacked in a way that makes sense for believers to live it out in their everyday lives. Everyday, that's the kind of discipleship we need, not just a Sunday or events driven relationship with Christ but a real, authentic, cross shaped life that brings glory to God. James has written the book that we all need, one that helps us to be true disciples of Jesus.

—**Josh Kelsey,** *Lead Pastor, FOUNT. NYC. PARIS. BERLIN (formerly C3.NYC)*

# AN INVITATION TO FOLLOW
## A PRACTICAL GUIDE TO DISCIPLESHIP

JAMES MURRAY

Ark House Press
arkhousepress.com

© 2023 JAMES MURRAY

All rights reserved. Apart from any fair dealing for the purpose of study, research, criticism, or review, as permitted under the Copyright Act, no part may be reproduced by any process without written permission.

Scriptures taken from the Holy Bible, New International Version®, NIV®. Copyright © 1973, 1978, 1984, 2011 by Biblica, Inc.™ Used by permission of Zondervan. All rights reserved worldwide. www.zondervan.com The "NIV" and "New International Version" are trademarks registered in the United States Patent and Trademark Office by Biblica, Inc.™

*Some names and identifying details have been changed to protect the privacy of individuals.*

Cataloguing in Publication Data:
Title: AN INVITATION TO FOLLOW
ISBN: 978-0-6459673-2-6 (pbk)
Subjects: REL108010 [RELIGION / Christian Church / Growth]; REL108030 [RELIGION / Christian Living / Leadership & Mentoring]; REL023000 [RELIGION / Christian Ministry / Discipleship];

Design by initiateagency.com

# CONTENTS

ABOUT THE AUTHOR ................................................................... vii

A CHANGE IS NEEDED ................................................................ ix

BEFORE YOU READ ..................................................................... xii
A Note to Jesus Followers ............................................................ xii
A Note to Church Pastors and Leaders ..................................... xiv

Chapter 1 - What Does It Mean To Be A Disciple? ...................... 1
Chapter 2 - Foundations and the Divine Order ............................ 7
Chapter 3 - Practice Makes Progress ............................................ 12
Chapter 4 - FOUNDATIONS: The Father Heart of God ........... 28
Chapter 5 - FOUNDATIONS:
              The Work of Jesus on the Cross ............................. 39
Chapter 6 - FOUNDATIONS: The Person and Power
              of the Holy Spirit ..................................................... 50

FORMATION PRELUDE ............................................................. 62
Chapter 7 - FORMATION: Community Accountability ........... 63
Chapter 8 - FORMATION: Reflective Reading .......................... 76
Chapter 9 - FORMATION: Persistent Prayer ............................. 91
Chapter 10 - FORMATION: Total Stewardship ......................... 99
Chapter 11 - FORMATION: Sabbath ......................................... 106

CONTINUING PRELUDE .................................................................. 110
Chapter 12 - CONTINUING:
    The Kingdom Of Heaven ........................................... 112
Chapter 13 - CONTINUING: Pray For The Sick ..................... 117
Chapter 14 - CONTINUING: Dealing with the Demonic ......... 124
Chapter 15 - CONTINUING: Serve the Poor ........................... 130

COMMISSIONING PRELUDE ...................................................... 136
Chapter 16 - Help Others To Become Disciples. ....................... 137

EPILOGUE .................................................................................. 143
THANK YOUS ............................................................................ 146

# ABOUT THE AUTHOR

I was born and raised in Sydney, Australia. My wife, Alanna, and I have four amazing children. I am passionate about the local church and have invested more than twenty years in full time church ministry - from high school pastor, to youth pastor, young adults pastor, church planter and now serving as lead pastor.

I have a deep desire to see people come to know and follow Jesus, unlocking the fullness of life that God wants for them. My heart is to serve and help local church pastors and have written two books, *Young and Free* and *Strictly Inclusive*. My hope with *An Invitation to a Journey - a Practical Guide to Discipleship* is to continue to encourage followers of Jesus, to support and inspire them towards living the abundant life Jesus came to give them.

# A CHANGE IS NEEDED

Richard Foster said:

> "Discipleship is not about a program or an event. It's about a relationship that transforms lives."

I grew up in church for the majority of my life, and I am incredibly grateful for that experience. However, in 2019, I found myself in a dark place in my Christian walk. I was frustrated and confused about the state of the church. Is Christianity merely a Sunday event? Is Christianity confined to a program on Sundays? Is it solely about expending energy and effort to encourage Christians to attend and engage in a Sunday service, with the hope of bringing their unchurched friends? Is it merely an internal belief that lacks impact on the outside world? Is a church's success solely determined by its size and the excellence of its weekend services? If I'm honest with myself, I must admit that, deep down, this is what I believed for many years. But what does it truly mean to be a Christian? What is the role of the church? My internal turmoil was signalling that a change was needed.

It was from this place of unrest that I rediscovered the invitation to a journey—the journey of discipleship. Through this book my desire is to help you understand what it truly means to be a disciple of Jesus and provide you with practical ways to follow Him. Every journey requires both a destination and a map. As Christians, our destination is to become more Christ-like, and the map guiding us on this journey is that of discipleship. It is a journey towards a transformed life.

What we need to admit is that the consumerist culture of the world around us has crept into the church. We see the church as a service designed to meet the felt needs of its members and while that is partly true, we need to come back to what the church is and what it is intended to be. When you hear the word "church," you automatically think of a building, a place of worship on a Sunday, but the word "church" in the Bible is the Greek word "Ekklesia," which means 'Called-out ones.' When we read the stories of Jesus, we see him *calling out* to Matthew, Mark, Luke, John, and many others to come and follow him. Not just to join a Sunday church service, but to follow Him, to learn an entirely new way of life with God and with others. To be called out is an invitation to stand out. To learn how to live in this new kingdom of love, to be a city on a hill that can't be hidden, that will shine brightly with an example of Jesus, to be the salt of the earth that brings flavour to life and preserves against the corruption of our surrounding culture. If this doesn't sound like your current faith journey, then maybe you were like me and had settled for a watered-down version of the greatest invitation ever given: to follow Jesus into the journey of discipleship. When we look at the current state of the westernised church, we know a change is needed, but we also recognise that change is possible and on the other side of that change is a liberating, fulfilling, life changing reality of following Jesus.

# BEFORE YOU READ

## A Note to Jesus Followers

In a 2019 Barna group study of the (American) church, it revealed four different categories of people in and around the church.

### PRODIGALS OR EX-CHRISTIANS

Do not identify themselves as Christian despite having attended a Protestant or Catholic church as a child or teen, or had considered themselves to be Christian at some time.

### NOMADS OR LAPSED CHRISTIANS

Identify themselves as Christian but have not attended church in a long time. The vast majority of nomads haven't been involved with a faith community for six months or more.

### HABITUAL CHURCHGOERS

Describe themselves as Christian and have attended church at least once in the last month, yet do not have foundational core beliefs or behaviours associated with being an intentional, engaged disciple.

## Resilient Disciples

Are Christians who (1) attend church at least monthly and engage with their church more than just attending worship services; (2) trust firmly in the authority of the Bible; (3) are committed to Jesus personally and affirm He was crucified and raised from the dead to conquer sin and death; and (4) express desire to transform the broader society as an outcome of their faith.

Maybe you fall into one of the first three categories. My hope is that when you read this book, you would slowly but surely take gradual steps in your faith and that you eventually progress into the last category. A resilient disciple, someone who has a vibrant, passionate and liberating journey with Jesus.

There are so many ways you can read this book, but I want to encourage you towards the two best ways to read it:

- ❖ Don't rush through this book. Take your time at the end of each chapter to pause and reflect. Consider what it is saying and invite God into each step of the journey.
- ❖ With someone else who is also on the journey of wanting to follow Jesus in a greater way. Discipleship best happens in community and conversation. So invite someone to do this with you.

## A Note to Church Pastors and Leaders

In 2014, my wife Alanna and I started a church in the living room of our little red brick house in the southern suburbs of Sydney. We had such a passion and desire to do something great for God through our local church, but 6 years into the church I hit a dark place. I felt this deep inner gnawing, like something wasn't right in the church I was leading. I was tired of the game. I felt like all I was doing was trying to entertain Christians. I had a deep passion to reach people far from God, but I felt like most of my effort was going towards just trying to get Christians to show up and engage in church community. I thought to myself - if this is it, I don't think I want to be a church pastor anymore. But in the midst of the darkest moment, God led me to Matthew 11:28-30, it was Jesus' invitation:

> [28]"Come to me, all you who are weary and burdened, and I will give you rest. [29]Take my yoke upon you and learn from me, for I am gentle and humble in heart, and you will find rest for your souls. [30]For my yoke is easy and my burden is light."

I felt God impress on my heart, 'James, you have the right heart, but you are carrying the wrong yoke.' You see, a yoke wasn't just a timber farming apparatus, it was terminology used by a Rabbi to describe his way of viewing the scriptures and it was also an invitation to take on his way of living out the scriptures. What God was saying to me was 'James, your motives are good, but your way of doing church is wrong. I had created a Sunday-centric church and had neglected to do what Jesus asked me to do - to go and MAKE DISCIPLES. Jesus never asked us to grow a Sunday gathering, He asked us to make disciples.

The late great Timothy Keller said:

> *"Discipleship is not a sprint; it's a marathon. It's a lifelong journey of following Jesus and becoming more like Him each day."*

In this book, I do my best to create a practical guide on how to become and help others become disciples of Jesus.

Discipleship is not about an invitation to attend a church, it's far greater than that, it's an invitation to follow...

The statistics are simple. The ones who made it through the COVID disruption stronger in their walk and committed to the cause of Christ, were the ones who went in as disciples. The ones who surrendered to a daily call and committed to daily spiritual rhythms. Those that engaged in a consistent community, consistent in Kingdom sacrifice and servanthood. The disciples made it through the storm.

Sadly, many of the crowd didn't. We must re-align our church communities to the great commission to go make disciples. I want to encourage you with a few ways you can use this book:

- ❖ Do a Sunday sermon series and preach through each of the topics.

- ❖ Align your small groups to speak into each of the topics the following week in their groups.
- ❖ Go through the book with your staff and key leaders. Make it a journey you take together with the plan of your staff and leaders being able to do the same with others.

I want to encourage you as church leaders not to consider this a course you run once off, but a culture of discipleship you create in your church. Discipleship is slow, hard work, but it produces the greatest fruit. I love the local church and I hope this stirs your passion for discipleship and gives you a practical guide on how to do so.

# CHAPTER 1

## What Does It Mean To Be A Disciple?

> *"One day as Jesus was walking along the shore of the Sea of Galilee, he saw two brothers— Simon, also called Peter, and Andrew—throwing a net into the water, for they fished for a living. 19 Jesus called out to them, "Come, follow me, and I will show you how to fish for people!" 20 And they left their nets at once and followed him."* (Matthew 4:18-20)

It was the year 1999 and I had just finished high school. I was at my year 12 formal and I wore a particularly nice safari suit (fashion trends always make a full circle). We danced to Prince's *'Tonight we're gonna party like it's 1999'* and as the night wore on, I realised - I was about to step into the 'real world' and it was time to consider my future more seriously.

What was I going to do with my life? What did I want to accomplish? I was unsure. Someone suggested I get into a trade, maybe try my hand at carpentry. Why not? It seemed easy enough. Accessible, doable. All I needed to do was commit to the process. How hard could it be? So in the hot Australian summer of 2000, I began a carpentry apprenticeship.

I would show up daily just before 7am to start learning the craft of building houses. The work and the skills were foreign to me and demanded more effort than I expected. But I committed the next few years to watching, listening, learning and practising the skill of carpentry and slowly but surely, what was once foreign became muscle memory. I was no longer simply learning the skill of carpentry, I was becoming a carpenter.

What does this have to do with discipleship? A whole lot.

The word "disciple" is not used in our modern day vernacular but was commonplace in ancient times to describe a category of people. In Hebrew, these people were referred to as *Talmid* and in Greek, *mathētés,* both of which translates to student or apprentice. In both these cultures, people often aimed to be disciples of notable leaders to learn and develop in their field. In ancient Greek society, students of philosophy longed to be a disciple or an apprentice of one of the great minds of their time - like Plato or Socrates. In Jewish society, it was an extremely honorable thing to become a disciple of a Rabbi. From five to six years of age, young Jewish boys and girls would go to synagogue school, known as 'Bet Sefer' (House of the Book) to learn the Torah which is the first five books of the Old Testament. At 10-14 years, the good students would go on to secondary school called 'Bet Talmud' (House of learning). The students that didn't get to that point would take on the family trade, like a farmer or a fisherman. For those successful in Bet Talmud, they would progress to the 'Bet Midrash' (House of Study). Very few students made it that far. If they did, there was a high chance that a Rabbi, after a series of intense probing questions about the Torah, would then say to the student, 'Come, follow me and be my disciples.' So the exhaustive process shows that this was no small feat and how huge an honour it was to accomplish.

While the word disciple means both student and apprentice, apprentice is more helpful to our modern day context because of all that it encompasses. The word student is great, but it takes us back to school and makes us think of textbooks and classrooms, habits of recall and rote learning that we associate with passing an exam. Meanwhile, an apprentice gives us the impression of, not just learning, but doing, active participation and hands-on practical experience. I believe this word alone can give us a radically new perspective around discipleship. So, as we journey through this book, remember this:

**DISCIPLE** = APPRENTICE TO JESUS

I want you to see yourself not just as a student learning knowledge about Jesus and His way of life, but as an apprentice, ultimately learning from Jesus so that you can live and do life the way He did.

Before we move on, here are some thoughts about what discipleship truly encompasses:

## 1. Discipleship is a choice

Jesus doesn't command you to be His disciple, it's a choice you must make. A teacher can approach a student and invite them to learn from them, but ultimately it's the student who chooses the teacher. Jesus invited plenty of people to be His disciple yet many of them said no. Crazy, right? Why would anyone reject Jesus' invitation? Because we want to be our own teacher - or even boss. We naturally prefer to call the shots in our own life or we want Jesus to follow us and help us fulfil our personal plans and agenda.

But to follow Jesus is to do exactly that, to follow. That means *we* don't take the lead, He does. Until you make this choice, discipleship or apprenticeship under Jesus will never be as fruitful as it should be. Jesus has given you the invitation, and you must choose to follow or not.

## 2. Discipleship is not just a confession of faith, but a commitment to follow

There is a big difference between belief and discipleship. Belief or faith in Jesus is the doorway into a new life in Christ. Discipleship is the embodiment of what comes after belief. Jesus asks us, not just to believe, but to follow Him and His way. Many people sit in church today who believe in Jesus, His death and resurrection, and that He is the Son of God - and that is amazing. But there is so much more to the story. This belief, faith or trust should develop into something that shapes the way we live and change our lifestyle! To clarify, faith pleases God. This is not intended to be a guilt trip forcing you to do things to please God. As the Apostle Paul wrote, *"The righteous will live by faith."* (Rom 1:17). But faith in Jesus is a filter we now pour our life through. We trust Him to save us and we trust Him to lead us as we live out this new life of salvation. We must commit not just to believe, but trust, obey and follow.

## 3. Discipleship is not leadership

For the last two decades, leadership has been a major focus in the western church. I think a big reason for this is because the local Sunday service became a more attractional gathering point. And to run a big or even average-sized, volunteer-driven organisation requires people and leadership. Leadership to lead teams, create culture, raise up future leaders etc. And this in itself is not bad. Leadership is a spiritual gift needed by and given to the church. However, somewhere along the way, I believe we confused leadership for discipleship. We hoped that, in the process of raising up these great leaders, disciples would be made, but for the most part, they weren't.

While leadership skills rose, spiritual maturity plummeted. I truly don't believe this happened intentionally - we just lost sight of what mattered most; making disciples. Now this does not mean we should swing the pendulum totally away from leadership development, because leaders are desperately needed in the life of a church. In fact, Jesus had more than twelve disciples, in the book of Luke He sent out 72 disciples (Luke 10:1), but He had 12 He brought closer, not just to teach them how to live like

He lived, but to teach them how to lead like He led and go on to lead as Apostles in the New Testament church.

In my opinion, Jesus had a very clear distinction between a disciple and a leader. Both were needed, but let's not confuse the two. A disciple is someone learning how to grow in spiritual maturity, and a leader is learning how to steward and lead Jesus' church well.

When Jesus gave the great commission to His disciples, He said "Go and make apprentices of me." We now know what an apprentice is, but what does apprenticeship to Jesus look like? And how do we help others with their apprenticeship? While Jesus didn't give us a ten step program, His life and the life of His disciples will shed some light on what His apprenticeship program would look like. So let's respond to His invitation to follow and begin our apprenticeship.

## PAUSE AND REFLECT:

- ❖ If discipleship is like an apprenticeship, how does that change the way you view each day following Jesus?
- ❖ In what areas do you feel like you are following Jesus vs trying to make Jesus follow you?

## A PRAYER:

*"Jesus, I have heard your invitation to follow You and apprentice under You. I admit much of me would prefer to be the one leading and controlling my own life, but today I am saying yes to Your invitation to follow. I choose to be Your disciple. Amen."*

CHAPTER 2

# Foundations and the Divine Order

*"18 Jesus came and told his disciples, "I have been given all authority in heaven and on earth. 19 Therefore, go and make disciples of all the nations, baptising them in the name of the Father and the Son and the Holy Spirit. 20 Teach these new disciples to obey all the commands I have given you. And be sure of this: I am with you always, even to the end of the age." (Matthew 28:18-20)*

Have you heard of Bonanno Pisano? He was a twelfth century artist who decided to try his luck at architecture. His first assignment was to build a beautiful bell tower that would sit adjacent to the town's cathedral. The construction began and you could only imagine how proud Bonanno must have been knowing this tower would stand as a reminder of his architectural prowess. Construction began and, as they reached the third story of what would be an eight story tower, they noticed the building starting to lean. Instead of starting again they decided to counterbalance the tower by adding more weight on the opposite side in the hopes that it would course correct, but it didn't work. On completion, the bell tower had an incredibly noticeable lean, which earned it the name, 'Leaning Tower Of Pisa'. But the question we must ask is, why does it lean? Well, they built the 55m-high tower, with only a 3m-deep foundation. To make matters worse they built it on a culmination of clay and sand, a notoriously unstable material. The moral of the story, *foundations matter.*

When we build a house, or any kind of structure, it is important to build on a solid and firm foundation. If we don't, the entire structure will be unsupported. It may begin to lean, sink and eventually collapse. Think about the Leaning Tower of Pisa. It leans because the foundations were not built correctly. They didn't invest the time and effort into using the right information to build a solid and deep foundation. And generations later, we see the after effects of what may well have been perceived as a minor oversight. The lean of the tower could have been avoided relatively easily, but they neglected to give proper attention to the foundations. If you want to build right, you need to get the foundations right.

Many people live their life with a lean because the foundations of their life aren't built correctly. Just like a building needs a strong foundation, so do we to withstand the temptations and storms of life. If we don't pay attention to our foundations we will not grow or progress as God intended. When we build strong foundations, we are built to last.

# FOUNDATIONS AND THE DIVINE ORDER

Here are three truths about foundations:

1. You can't build properly without foundations.
2. Foundations need to be strong.
3. You don't ever remove your foundations.

We need to come back to the foundations of our Christianity. If we don't, we may live our lives with a lean. If we find that our life isn't as stable as we would like it to be, it may be because our foundations are not correct. I believe that true and lasting change starts in the foundations.

## What are the foundations of our faith?

Years ago I was reading Jesus' great commission in Matthew 28, and I read the words:

> *"Therefore, go and make disciples of all the nations, baptising them in the name of the **Father** and the **Son** and the **Holy Spirit**." - Matthew 28:19 (emphasis added)*

I had read this hundreds of times and I'd never seen it before. A divine order that we must have as the foundation of our faith. Allow me to explain. When Jesus said baptise them, He used the Greek word *baptízō* which means to fully immerse or submerge. This speaks to the literal act of water baptism for those who would follow Jesus, but it's not just a baptism into a body of water, it's a baptism into a new reality. The reality of the Triune God or the trinity. To me Jesus wanted His followers to be immersed in the reality of:

- ❖ The Father = The Father heart of God.
- ❖ The Son = The finished work of Jesus on the cross
- ❖ The Holy Spirit = The person and the power of the Holy Spirit.

To establish the correct foundation in our faith, we must be exposed to this divine order, specifically in that order. We must understand that it was in the Father's heart that the plan for salvation and relationship began, through the Son's work on the cross that this salvation and relationship was made possible and through the Holy Spirit that we can now live, enjoy and remain connected to this amazing new life with God. You see, this is the foundation of our faith. This is what we build this new life of discipleship on.

As Christians we need to continually come back to these three foundations and build our lives on them. As you continue through this book, I want you not just to consider these foundations, but to remind yourself daily of this new reality, immerse yourself in them. Let it shape the way you view God.

## PAUSE AND REFLECT:

- ❖ What do you think the foundations of your life have been built on? Is there anything there that isn't God, that isn't going to help you build a strong healthy future?

❖ Think about what your faith is built on. Is it a shallow or deep understanding of the Father, Son and Holy Spirit? Make a decision as you move forward throughout this book that you are going to go deeper into the foundations of faith.

## A PRAYER:

*"Father, Son and Holy Spirit I open myself up to you. I want to know you in a deeper way. Open the eyes of my heart to understand and experience The Fathers heart, the finished work of Jesus on the cross and the person and power of the Holy Spirit. Amen."*

# CHAPTER 3

## Practice Makes Progress

*7.... train yourself to be godly. 8 For physical training is of some value, but godliness has value for all things, holding promise for both the present life and the life to come. 9 This is a trustworthy saying that deserves full acceptance. 10 That is why we labor and strive, because we have put our hope in the living God, who is the Savior of all people, and especially of those who believe. (1 Timothy 4:7-8)*

Have you ever had an idea that seemed great at the time, only to regret it later?

I've had plenty. I once had the idea to ride a bicycle from Sydney to Canberra to raise money for a local Salvation Army initiative. I thought to myself, how hard could it be? I've been riding a bike since I was three years old! So I neglected to do a pretty important thing when it comes to a three day, 350 km ride (218 miles for my American friends). I neglected to *train* for the ride and to be honest, I didn't want to. Less than one hour into the ride, my legs were burning and my hopes of achieving this accomplishment were quickly diminishing. I kept thinking to myself, 'Man, I massively underestimated what it would take to do this.'

The moral of the story, I wanted the end result, but I didn't want to put in the work required.

Isn't this true of life? We want more money, but we want to work less. We want an amazing marriage, but we don't give time to invest into it. We want an amazing body, but we want to eat whatever we want and not exercise too much.

If we are honest this is also true when it comes to our faith. We want an amazing church community, but don't want to spend time with people. We want all of God's blessings, but we don't want all of God's commandments. We want all God has to offer, but we don't want to offer God our all. We want Godly outcomes, but we neglect Godly input.

Somewhere along the way we have concluded that to be a disciple of Jesus is an effortless journey. We just sit in a church service on a Sunday and hopefully, we become more Christ-like. But I'm sorry to say, it's not entirely true, input and effort are required.

Let me put it this way, God's grace & salvation are passive - we don't do anything to earn it, it is a gift of God, we just believe (Ephesians 2:8-9). But God's transformation in our lives is active. We must participate in His transforming work in our lives, and the greatest way to progress in your faith is to practise your faith.

Imagine someone is given a free gym membership, they walk into their new found fitness community and they are excited about the idea of getting fit and into shape. They show up every week, but months and months go by, and they haven't seen any physical progress. They approach one of the gym trainers and complain about their lack of transformation. To which they respond,

"I'm sorry to hear that, what exercises have you been doing?" or "What gym classes have you been attending?"

"Exercise? Gym classes?" they exclaim, "You're telling me I have to do something? Just being in the gym isn't enough?"

I know what you're thinking, this person is not the sharpest crayon in the box but this is how many people view their Christianity. I show up to church, and by mere attendance in a faith community, my life will be transformed. But that's not how it works.

<u>When it comes to our transformation:</u>
<u>Practice makes progress.</u>

Just like going to the gym, the more you put into practice the teachings and lifestyle of Jesus, the more you will progress. The beautiful thing is, unlike the gym, you don't operate in your own effort. You have the Holy Spirit working with you and inside you as you take the journey.

In 1 Timothy 4:7-8 Paul is writing to his young protege and encourages him in a few things I believe really deserve our attention:

- → V7 - *"train yourself to be **godly**."*
- → V8 - *"..godliness has value for all things, holding promise for both the present life and the life to come."*

Paul uses the word *'godly'*, as soon as we see that word, it's easy to feel a little deflated or challenged by it because not many of us would feel very *'godly.'* But the word godly means 'god-like', in other words, you are aspiring to be more like your heavenly father. I have four kids, and every now and then people will come up to me and say "your boy or your daughter is so much like you". What they mean by that is that my kids have, by relationship and proximity, picked up my characteristics. They aren't me, but they are behaving like me. This is what it means to be goldy. In times past, people would call this *'theosis'* or *'deification'* which means becoming like God or restoring you to your God made image. You have a God made image, that sin has distorted and warped.

God, by His grace, and you, through your obedience, are working at restoring the part of you that longs to be like your creator. The light and salt He always intended for you to be. But this requires effort. Paul says you need to train yourself to be Godly. Notice how he says *"godliness has value"* and *"holding promise in this life and the one to come."* Paul is saying to pursue or train for godliness isn't about struggling this side of eternity and one day in heaven you will reap a reward. He is saying this has benefits now! If you lived and handled your everyday life more like Jesus, would your life be more beneficial and enjoyable? The answer is obvious. YES. Paul is saying that training in godliness leads you to live more like Jesus and in turn, you will experience more of the abundant life and liberty of God, not a perfect life void of problems and pain, but a progressing life. So how do we practise and progress in our faith?

I believe there are four things we should consider.

- # **Position**
- # **Practice**
- # **Persistence**
- # **People**

## POSITION:

Know where you are at and know where you want to go. It's really hard to get anywhere if you don't know where you are. Most shopping malls have large digital maps where you can type in what shop you are looking for and it draws a directional line from where you are to where the shop is. If it just told you where the shop was but neglected to show you where you were, you would get frustrated and lost. I believe many people on their spiritual journey are like that. They long to grow and mature in their faith but they don't know where they are or how to get there. So how do you discover your position on the spiritual journey?

While there are many stages of faith, I once heard someone say it like this.

**Curious Stage**
You are interested in faith. Maybe a co-worker or a friend is a christian and the way they lived or talked about their faith made you curious. Those in the curious stage are yet to believe and put their trust in Jesus.

**Come and See Stage**
You want to believe, but you're not totally sure. You have doubts, but you are now showing up to church or a group setting to explore more about the person of Jesus and the Christian faith.

**Come and Follow Stage**
You believe and have a basic understanding of following Jesus. You would call yourself a christian, but you are still yet to experience deeper levels of intimacy and transformation in your faith.

**Be With Me Stage**
You are getting a greater desire to know God and you find yourself enjoying time alone with Him. Worship and His word have taken a new depth in your life.

**Abide in Me Stage**
You feel deeply connected to God. You've reached a level of trust, dependence and inti-

macy with God and you are more conscious of Him in your everyday life. You are not perfect but you have grown significantly in your transformation journey, you notice it and others notice it too.

Out of these five stages. which one are you at and where would you like to be? Once you know your position it's a lot easier to make progress. A beautiful thing to remember is that God doesn't stay at a distance, but He meets you on whichever step you are on.

## PRACTICE:

What you do consistently is who you are becoming. You are not the byproduct of your goals and intentions. You are the byproduct of your habits, or your practices. A great athlete can have natural talent, but what makes a great athlete is the practice they put in. I know we have touched on this already, but we must understand that the habits or choices we are making consistently are shaping our spiritual formation.

In his book 'Mere Christianity' C.S. Lewis puts it like this:

> *"Every time you make a choice you are turning the central part of you, the part of you that chooses, into something a little different from what it was before. And taking your life as a whole, with all your innumerable choices, all your life long, you are slowly turning this central thing either into a*

> *heavenly creature or into a hellish creature: either into a creature that is in harmony with God, with others, and with self, or else into one that is in a state of war and hatred with God, and with its fellow-creatures, and with itself."*

He is saying your consistent choices are changing the trajectory of your transformation, both for good and for bad. In other words all your little choices matter. But how do we direct our choices? Deep down inside we all want to do what is good. But in the heat of temptation our sin-distorted desires can sometimes overtake us. This is where your habits or practices really kick in. For example, for my age and height I used to be pretty overweight. Let's just say it was hard to hide the silhouette of my muffin tops. I was overweight because I loved eating junk food. Then one day I had a rude shock as I looked at a photo of me with one of my children. My initial thought was 'Who is that chubby guy holding my kid?' Only to quickly realise it was me. It was then I made a decision that I needed to change so I went to a personal trainer and he told me that to change my weight, I didn't need to go on a diet, I needed to change my lifestyle.

I've discovered that a majority of people desire to change, but they treat christianity like a diet. They make a decision to abstain from certain behaviours, and they make progress. But just like a diet, once they've achieved their goal weight or fitness, they relax again and think to themselves, *I've been pretty good, I should treat myself to one of my old guilty pleasures.*

And slowly but surely the discipline wanes and they end up back where they started, guilt kicks in and motivates them to either go back on the diet or give up completely. I've seen many people's faith journeys and it looks just like this. The reason why is because they see christianity as a diet, but Christianity isn't an invitation to a diet - it goes beyond restrictions, rules and hyper awareness of the things that you consume. It is an invitation to embed the things of God into every facet of who you are, embodying the things of God that ultimately change your lifestyle.

How do you create a new lifestyle? You create new practices or perhaps a better word is habits. Why? Because what you do consistently is who you are becoming. We all have habits, and those habits are shaping who we are, but here is a question I want you to consider:

> *What habits do you have that are helping you grow in your relationship with God?*

My wife, Alanna, enjoys gardening, she finds it therapeutic. I, on the other hand, prefer to torture myself playing this brutal game called golf, but I digress. In our backyard, there was a white panel fence that looked nice enough as it was, but she thought we could make it a bit more appealing. So she planted some ivy vine seeds at the base of the fence. It slowly started to grow but she didn't want it to grow along the ground, she wanted it to cover the entire fence. She strung a thin metal wire across the fence that enables the vine to easily climb the fence. If you were to come to our house today, you wouldn't see a white panel fence. All you can see now is a beautiful lush, green ivy wall. Point of the story:

> *She didn't make the vine grow, she just created a way for it to grow best.*

Holy habits or spiritual practices in and of themselves are not your faith - they are just a way to help your faith grow best. The point isn't just to read your bible, pray, go to church, serve others. They are just a means to an end. What is that end? A deeper, more abiding relationship with Jesus. There is a saying that practice makes perfect, well let me relieve some pressure, you won't be perfect in all these practices. However I do want you to know this, practice makes progress. They will help you to progress.

What are some of the best practices? A majority of this book is helping you with exactly that so keep on reading.

## PERSISTENCE:

A few years ago, I picked up my eldest boy from school and I asked how his day was. He told me he actually had a good day and that he had just got his marks back from a recent maths test. Much like his father, maths wasn't his strong point, so I asked him how he went. He said he actually did really well!

"Really?" I replied, "That's great! What did you do differently?" To which he replied. "Well, I just tried."

One of the big things I think we have missed in our modern day westernised church culture, is that while God's love, grace and salvation are free, Gods transforming work in our lives requires us to put in persistent effort.

Paul alludes to this in his letter to the Galatian church:

> *⁷ Do not be deceived: God cannot be mocked. A man reaps what he sows. ⁸ Whoever sows to please their flesh, from the flesh will reap destruction; whoever sows to please the Spirit, from the Spirit will reap eternal life. ⁹ Let us not become weary in doing good, for at the proper time we will reap a harvest if we do not give up. - (Galatians 6:7-9)*

Paul uses an agricultural farming analogy to describe how transformation works. A few thoughts from the scripture:

### *"God cannot be mocked. A man reaps what he sows."*

Paul is saying that God has put a law in place very much like the law of gravity. What you sow you will reap, what you put in you will get out, both for good and for bad. People can try to mock God by doing whatever they want, but just like a person defying the law of gravity by jumping out of a plane without a parachute, that person will reap a confronting reality called the ground. 'Sowing and reaping' isn't just a principle, it's a God established law. You are getting out what you are putting in.

## *"Whoever sows to please their flesh, from the flesh will reap destruction"*

Paul goes on to use the word flesh. The Greek word for flesh is the word *sárx*.

The *sárx* is our sinful nature, or the sin-desiring aspect of our being. He says that if you keep sowing to the sin-desiring aspect of your being, you will reap destruction. In other words, it really *sárx* to live that way (I know, horrible Dad joke, but I needed to get your attention again. Forgive me). He is addressing the destructive patterns we keep reinforcing in our lives through our sinful habits. Easy example: If you keep looking at pornography on the internet, if you keep feeding that lustful desire, you will bring destruction to the deep intimacy that you are designed to have with a real person, not a person on screen, in the covenant relationship of marriage.

## *"Whoever sows to please the Spirit, from the Spirit will reap eternal life."*

Paul says there is a better alternative. Sowing to please the Spirit. He speaks to those Holy habits, some of which we will cover in this book. Things that please God, like worship and prayer. When you create habits like this, you will reap eternal life. Eternal life isn't just about living for eternity with Jesus one day; he is speaking about eternal life now. I believe eternal life speaks to the life Jesus spoke of in John 10:10, Life and life in abundance. The Greek word for 'life' is *zóé* which means absolute fullness, genuine or blessed. Paul is saying when you persist in sowing into your spiritual life, that's where you are truly going to experience life.

*"Let us not become weary in doing good, for at the proper time we will reap a harvest if we do not give up."*

Now this part is really important. Paul knows that this is not an easy path to walk. In fact, he says sometimes you are going to feel a little weary, a little tired, but just like an olympic runner doing a race, he reminds us that there is that prize of eternal life at the end. So don't give up. This is really important because as you take the journey of following Jesus, of apprenticing under him, there will be times where it gets hard. You will have to say no to things that you used to easily say yes to. You are going to have to go against the flow of the world around you, but don't give up! Eternal life is coming!

## PEOPLE:

I once heard a story about one of my favourite theologians, D.L.Moody. After preaching at a church event, he was approached by a wealthy businessman who had attended the event and asked if he would speak to him in private. He agreed and they went into a side room of the church. They sat in two armchairs, facing the fire and the businessman began to say how much he enjoyed D.L.Moody's sermons but there was one part of his orthodoxy he didn't quite agree with. He didn't believe you needed a church community to follow Jesus. In fact it is probably better alone.

D.L.Moody didn't say anything. He just got up from his chair, walked over to the fireplace, grabbed the fire stoker and pulled a red hot coal from the fire and placed it onto the ceramic surface in front and stared. The man looked at him, still waiting for a response but only saw D.L's unbroken gaze on the piece of coal. They both proceeded to stare at the coal, and slowly but surely the red hot coal became dimmer and dimmer until the light and heat had gone out of it. D.L. Moody, still not saying a word, looked back at him. To which the man said, *I get your point.*

You see people aren't an optional extra for our journey of transformation, they are a necessity!

Author M.Robert.Mulholland Jr, in his book 'Invitation to a journey' wrote:

> "We can no longer be formed in the image of Christ outside of corporate spirituality than a coal can continue to burn bright outside of the fire... When we don't feel like worshipping, the community should carry us along in its worship. When we can't seem to pray, community prayer should enfold us. When the scripture seems closed for us, the community should keep on reading, affirming and incarnating it around us."

We need each other. Church community is from God to help us, to shoulder with us in our journey to follow Jesus. Jude 1:20 says:

> "But you, dear friends, must build each other up in your most holy faith..."

We have a responsibility to each other. To build each other up in faith, to come together like coals in a fire and keep each other burning bright in the lifestyle of Jesus we have chosen to live. I implore you, as you take the journey of reading and applying this book, don't do it alone. Do it with someone else. There is a reason why Jesus sent his disciples out in groups of two (Mark 6:7). Our faith burns brighter and stronger when we live it out together.

So now we are ready. The stage has been set. You know now what it means to be a disciple. You know that practice makes progress. So let's begin first by going deeper into the divine order of the foundations of our faith. Foundations are essential to the future-you that God is building.

## **PAUSE AND REFLECT:**

- ❖ **Position** - Where are you on the spiritual spectrum? Discover where you are and where you want to go. Be honest, God will meet you there.
- ❖ **Practice** - We will discover more about practices in the coming chapters, but what small thing can you commit to start doing to create some Holy Habits in your life? (e.g. getting up a bit earlier to pray each day, listening to a worship song each morning on the way to work,etc)
- ❖ **Persistence** - What are you sowing into right now that you know is destructive to who God is calling you to be? Bring it into the light, repent of it and ask for God's strength to help you break that habit and help you to create new Holy Habits.
- ❖ **People** - Who can you reach out to and include on this journey of discipleship? Bring them in on the journey, do it together. Help and encourage one another.

## A PRAYER:

*"Father, I come before You today and acknowledge that I am not where I want to be, but I want to progress on my journey of change. Would You shape my desires and habits so that I can go deeper into the reality of who You are and who You are calling me to be. I love You and I trust You with my journey. Amen.*

# CHAPTER 4

• • • ○ • • •

# FOUNDATIONS:
# The Father Heart of God

I want to start this chapter with a thought provoking quote from A.W. Tozer from his brilliant book *'The Knowledge of the Holy'*:

> *"What comes into our minds when we think about God is the most important thing about us...We tend by a secret law of the soul to move toward our mental image of God... a right conception of God is basic not only to systematic theology but to practical christian living as well. It is to worship what the foundation is to the temple; where it is inadequate or out of plumb the whole structure must sooner or later collapse."*

Basically what Tozer is saying is the way you see God is how you will approach Him.

This may seem off topic, but let me ask you a question - why did Jesus come to earth? Most people would say the reason was to die on the cross, show us the way to live, and to demonstrate miracles and healing. And all of that is true. But at the beginning of the Gospel of John, Jesus tells us He came to make the Father known, to reveal Him (John 1:18). Everything Jesus did and said was pointing us to, and getting our attention on the Father. Jesus wanted us to understand the Father Heart of God. Prior to Jesus, there was plenty of religion but Jesus wanted us to know who God was and what He was like. So Jesus put on flesh and said I'm going to show you what He thinks about you, how He feels about you and how He acts towards you. He came to make the Father known.

In the gospel of Luke, Jesus tells the parable of the Prodigal Son (Luke 15:11-24).

The word parable in the Greek is the word *parabolē* which means: a comparison. Another definition of the parable is 'an earthly story with a heavenly meaning', a parable has also been described as a 'mirror and a window'. It's a mirror that causes you to look at yourself, and a window through which we see God and His truth more clearly.' but I like this definition the most:

> *A parable is like a mental "time bomb" designed to be unforgettable and then to explode into meaning for those who are serious about listening to the Lord*

How good is that? I am hoping that this parable becomes like a time bomb in your soul that explodes into a greater understanding of the Father heart of God.

Allow me to give you a quick overview of the story. In the story the son does not want to wait for the father to die before he receives his inheritance. He wants to go and party and live the life he wants. Amazingly, the father does not stop him, he lets him do it. He allows him to choose. Just as God has given us the free will to choose the direction of our life and whether we want Him in it or not. But the son realises after spending his inheritance and ending up in a pig pen that maybe this life is not so great after all and wants to return to the father. I really want to bring your attention to what the father does next in the story because it never fails to blow my mind:

> *"20....And while he was still a long way off, his father saw him coming. Filled with love and compassion, he ran to his son, embraced him, and kissed him. 21 His son said to him, 'Father, I have sinned against both heaven and you, and I am no longer worthy of being called your son.[b]' 22 "But his father said to the servants, 'Quick! Bring the finest robe in the house and put it on him. Get a ring for his finger and sandals for his feet. 23 And kill the calf we have been fattening. We must celebrate with a feast, 24 for this son of mine was dead and has now returned to life. He was lost, but now he is found." (Luke 15:20-24)*

This is part of the story I believe Jesus was really trying to get his listeners to pay attention to. He is using the parable to reveal the Father heart of God.

There are three important things from this parable that we can learn about the Father heart of God.

## 1. He Pursues You

We see all throughout the narrative of scripture that God is not a God who waits at a distance. He pursues us. He goes after us. He is a God who longs to be in a relationship with us. (Genesis 3:9, Psalm 139:7-8, Ezekiel 34:11, Revelation 3:20, to name a few).

> "...And while he was still a long way off, his father saw him coming. Filled with love and compassion, he ran to his son.." (Luke 15:20)

The father ran to him filled with LOVE and COMPASSION.

Some people think that God's pursuit of us is more like a police pursuit. He's coming after us because we have done something wrong, and He is coming to bring judgement. But this story does not reflect that. The scripture reflects a love pursuit. He's going after us filled with love and compassion. This was the energy fueling the pursuit of the father towards the son.
He pursues you with **LOVE**. The Greek word for this type of love is *agápe,* meaning 'one way, sacrificial, unconditional love.' This is the type of love the Father pursues you and I with. I love how Brennan Manning in his book '*The Ragamuffin Gospel*' put its:

> "I could more easily contain Niagara Falls in a teacup than I can comprehend the wild, uncontainable love of God."

God pursues you with a heart filled with love!

He pursues you with **COMPASSION**. The Greek word for compassion is *'splanchnízomai'* (pronounced 'Splunk-ne-zomai') which means 'a deep yearning to act on someone's behalf.' It's a deep care that motivates a person to help. Like a child falling over in a playground and badly hurting themselves, a loving parent won't stay at a distance and shout "Poor thing, that must have hurt". They get up and run toward the child, picking them up in their arms to hold them close in their pain. This is how the God of compassion pursues you!

The Book of Isaiah 30:18 says:

> *"Yet the Lord longs to be gracious to you; therefore he will rise up to show you compassion."*

Why would we run from a God who pursues us like that? We do this because we don't fully know and understand the Father heart of God. God's love is not a police pursuit, it's a love pursuit. We run from God because we think He's going to give us what we deserve. But we see through the story He doesn't ever give us what we deserve. He pursues you.

## 2. He Embraces You

> *"....he ran to his son, embraced him, and kissed him." (Luke 15:20)*

When Jesus was telling this story everyone would have been thinking he was going to run to him and beat him. A custom in Jewish tradition would have been to stone the son as he walked in for the disgrace he had brought to the family and to the village. But no, the father runs and he embraces and kisses his son. Many theologians believe this was to protect the son from the stoning. So the embrace doesn't just speak of affection, it speaks of protection.

He protects us from our accusers! The accusing voices in our heads that remind us of things we have done in our past, the Father throws His arms around us and covers us with forgiveness and protection.

Next he kisses him. The kiss was more than an act of affection. The kiss was an act of pardon. The kiss was the father acknowledging everything the son had done wrong and willingly choosing to forget it. *I'm going to pardon you.*

The book of Isaiah 55:7 says:

> *Let the wicked forsake their ways and their unrighteous thoughts. Let them turn to the Lord, and he will have mercy on them, and to our God, for he will **freely pardon.***

All the son needed to do, and all we need to do, is go to the Father. To repent, to turn, and the father, the Lord, did not and does not hesitate to freely pardon our sins.

So many people have neglected the Father' heart of God that says He will protect and pardon us. He is not holding us to our past anymore. We allow the past to continue to accuse us because we have forgotten the foundation that is the Father heart of God. Our past has been pardoned!

## 3. He Covers You

> *"21 His son said to him, 'Father, I have sinned against both heaven and you, and I am no longer worthy of being called your son. 22 "But his father said to the servants, 'Quick! Bring the finest robe in the house and put it on him. Get a ring for his finger and sandals for his feet." (Luke 15:21-22)*

The father places his finest robe on the son. This speaks of a covering. The son has spent his recent years working in a pig pen and is running to the father stinking of a pig sty. The father throws the finest robe over the mess. This tells us that God desires, not to judge your mess, but to cover it with His righteousness. (Don't worry we will cover this word 'righteous' in the next chapter on Jesus' work on the cross. It's extremely important.)

The Book of Isaiah 1:18 says:

> *"Come now, let's settle this," says the Lord. "Though your sins are like scarlet, I will make them as white as snow. Though they are red like crimson, I will make them as white as wool."*

The finest robe is symbolic of the righteousness of Jesus that is now given to us. This is what is referred to as 'Imputed righteousness'. It basically means Jesus lived a perfect, spotless, blemishless life and we have not. Imputed righteousness in simplest terms is Jesus saying 'Lets swap, your sinful life for my perfect, spotless, blemishless life.' It doesn't seem fair, does it? And you're right. That's why grace has often been referred to as *amazing*! And the more you reflect on the truth of how undeserving we are, the more amazing we realise grace is!

You see God's righteousness covers the most horrendous mistakes we've ever made. The finest robe in God's wardrobe is not riches, it's His righteousness. We are not seen for what we have done but for what Jesus has done for us. You are covered in His righteousness.

## 4. He Blesses You

> *22...Get a ring for his finger and sandals for his feet. 23 And kill the calf we have been fattening. We must celebrate with a feast, 24 for this son of mine was dead and has now returned to life. He was lost, but now he is found." (Luke 15:22-24)*

If we really understand all the things God has to do in order to bless us, we would be humbled by it because we realise how much we don't deserve it. The truth is we were broken, lost and messed up, but God's grace says I will bless you anyway. Let's slow the train down for a minute and really dive into the significance of the blessings the father gives the son.

## THE RING

The father in the story put a ring on the son which speaks to family and authority. The ring would have been like a family signet ring. When you wore that ring, people knew you were an intimate member of that family. The ring also symbolises authority. In ancient times you didn't sign legal documents or important transactions with a handwritten signature, instead you would pour melted wax onto the parchment and push the emblem or signet of the ring into the wax. If you had that ring, you were able to operate under and on behalf of the authority of the leader of the family, the father, or the king. When the son left the father's house originally he would have handed back this ring, as if to say, I no longer want to be under the authority, care or providence of the father. I want to be my own man, my own boss, my own king. But what is amazing is that when the son came back, the father didn't even hesitate to put the ring on his finger, he gave him his authority back. This means for us, as we come to the father he also gives us the ability to operate under his authority. Jon Tyson, a pastor in New York City, brilliantly said, *"Jesus didn't come to get God's authority back, he came to get our authority back."* God has never lost His authority, but sin and separation from God robbed us of ours, and the father longs to give it back. (There is so much more to say on this topic, but it will have to wait until chapter 12. Stay tuned)

## THE SANDALS

The sandals he placed on his feet speak of sonship. In ancient times slaves did not wear shoes, only the children of the house wore shoes. In the story the son's loose living had brought him to poverty. He had lost everything, even the shoes on his feet and the story tells us that he hired himself out to a local farmer to feed pigs. In other words he became a voluntary slave. Let me make a big statement, when Jesus came and died on the cross, He paid the penalty for sin. Once and for all, the debt for our sin has been paid. However, so many people are still trying to pay the debt for their sin on their own. Jesus paid for their sin and gave them the ability to be freed, but because they don't turn to Jesus, they remain slaves to sin, or voluntary slaves. It's their choice. The son in the story chooses to go back to the father, he thinks the father will probably make him a slave to pay off his debt, but the father quickly puts shoes on his feet, why? Because he was never meant to be a slave, he was always meant to be a son.

Paul writes in Romans 6:6:

> *"We are no longer slaves to sin."*

We are no longer a slave to our past, we are now sons and daughters of God.

## THE FEAST

The feast speaks of God's joy for you. When you turn to the father, he throws a party! A fattened calf in ancient times was the equivalent of an extremely expensive bottle of champagne saved for very special occasions. Some theologians believe the fattened calf speaks of the animal reserved for *Yōm Kippūr* which means 'Day of Atonement', an annual festival where Jewish people gathered to offer sacrifice to God for the atonement of sins.

It's almost as if Jesus is speaking into what would be His sacrifice for the atonement of our sins. Something He didn't do begrudgingly or out of duty but out of joy. As Hebrews 12:2 says:

*"For the joy set before him he endured the cross"*

This is an incredible insight into the joy of the father for his children. When God sees you, He is overjoyed!

The Father Heart of God is not something we move on from, it is something we move deeper into. Don't just read scripture to attain knowledge, allow it to show you the Father heart of God towards his children, which you are one of.

## PAUSE AND REFLECT:

- What does this parable tell you about the Father Heart of God?
- Take time to sit and consider your view of God, how do you see Him?
- Read the Luke 15 parables again and ask God to reveal His heart to you in a great way.

## A PRAYER:

*"God you are my loving father, I thank you for loving me. I don't think I will ever truly know the depths of your love, but I know I can discover and experience more of your love, reveal more of your love for me today. Help me to let that love become the foundation of my life. Amen."*

# CHAPTER 5

# FOUNDATIONS:
# The Work of Jesus on the Cross

When we look at a sign, symbol or logo, they have the ability to prompt a response in us. As soon as we look at it, it makes us think of something specific. It can initiate a desire or feeling in us simply because we see a symbol. For example, what do you think of when you see the Nike tick? You think 'Just do it'. What do you think when you see the golden arches of McDonald's? You think 'I'm lovin it' (and regretting it later), but when you see the symbol of the cross, what do you think?

For most people it would be a symbol of religion, a symbol of sorrow, it can even be just a fashion symbol. But when we fully understand the finished work of the cross, it should be a symbol that stirs up amazement, joy, freedom and liberation. Prior to Jesus' work on the cross, it was seen as a symbol of shame, humiliation and death, but after Jesus' work on the cross it became one of the greatest sources of joy for believers. It is something we look to and think 'that is where my hope lies'. This is what we hang our lives on. The cross wasn't just an event, it is a filter you are meant to see your entire life through.

Let me put it this way. One day I decided to go to the movies by myself (don't ask), I was running late and walked into a basically empty cinema. I sat down and stared up at the screen only to discover the screen was blurry and semi distorted. At first I thought the cinema projector lens was broken. I'm sometimes not the sharpest crayon in the box, but I eventually realised there was nothing wrong with the projector, it was in fact a 3D film and I had forgotten to grab the glasses required to see the movie correctly. Once I put them on, how radically different the picture appeared. The 3D lens caused it to come alive with depth and brilliance, it radically changed how I viewed what was once distorted. In a similar way when you think of the cross of Jesus, don't just see it as a historical event. See it as a lens through which you now view your past, present and future.

We need to allow the foundation of the cross to transform our past, our present, and our future. If we don't, we have "unfinished works" in our lives. But we must understand the finished work of the cross. The work of the cross is complete.

The apostle Paul said 1 Corinthians 2:2:

> *"For I resolved to know nothing while I was with you except Jesus Christ and him crucified."*

In other words, he made a deliberate decision to take everything to the cross and through the cross. He realised the power of what the cross did in his life and through his life. The cross changed him from a person of staunch legalism to a person of love and mercy. His security was no longer based on his religious performance but on Jesus' performance on his behalf. Instead of seeking change in his life from the outside in, the cross led him to experience change from the inside out. He went from a person who heaped religious oppression upon his followers, to a person who help lift the burden and lead people to the easy yoke of Jesus. Safe to say it had ramifications on Paul's past, on his present and on his future. It transformed his life and it has the power to transform yours.

## 1. How does the cross change the way I see my past?

**The cross can't change the events of the past, but it does change the effects of the past.**

Here is what I have found: *Before Jesus takes you forward, He will often take you backwards.* Who you are today has been largely shaped by your past. Some psychologists refer to this idea as 'Sovereign Foundations'. They believe that during your formative years, mainly between the ages of 0-18, things that have happened in your life have played a part in forming who you are today. Some of these things may have been intentional or unintentional, some learnt behaviours, some observed behaviours, good, bad and neutral moments - they've all played their role in shaping you. I truly believe this. Your past matters. It is unwise to go charging into the future without first inspecting your past. The past should not be ignored but explored. We should explore it with the lens of the cross.

Have you ever heard of Spelunking? Spelunking is cave exploration, sometimes underwater! Scuba divers will explore the underwater caves hidden at the base of a mountain (a claustrophobic nightmare). They dive down into these deep dark caves and canyons and shine a light on places unexplored by mankind. This is what Jesus longs to do within you. To dive deep into the dark unexplored places of your past and shine the light of His love, grace and healing into the parts of our past we would prefer to ignore. As we trust Him in the process we discover that He doesn't shine a light on your past to expose and shame you, but to liberate you. As the Apostle Paul declares in 2 Corinthians 3:17:

*"Where the spirit of the Lord is there is freedom."*

The journey requires courage, but the end result is well worth it. The *events* of the past cannot be changed, but the *effects* of the past can. The healing power of the cross can redeem the sovereign foundations and help you build a better future. Explore it with Jesus and allow Him to go back into your past and experience the freedom it brings

**The cross liberates us from the penalty of the sins of our past**

We need to understand the weight of this. The cross will never be of value to us until we realise how bad we were. God cannot be a god of love, without also being a god of justice. The bible says we were all fallen. The book of Romans states there is not one righteous person (Romans 3:10). We need to realise our brokenness to experience the liberation the cross brings.

You see the Gospel is not just good advice, the gospel is good news! When we bring our past to Jesus we recognise we all have a past. We all have issues. Prior to accepting Jesus the bible says we were at war with God. We were His enemy and we were in debt to God. We had the debt of sin. Paul the Apostle writes in Romans 6:23:

> *"For the wages of sin is death, but the free gift of God is eternal life through Christ Jesus our Lord."*

In 2005 nine Australians entered the city of Bali, not with the intention of a vacation, but to smuggle drugs out of Bali into Australia. The well known penalty for smuggling drugs in or out of Indonesia was death. Knowing this, they risked it and were caught by the Balinese police. Seven were sentenced to prison and two of the nine were sentenced to death by firing squad, a very sad and tragic end. But now imagine these two men standing before the judge as the gavel comes down as he declares the words 'guilty!' But instead of the men going to the firing squad that same judge got down from his bench and stood in front of the firing squad taking the penalty for the men, and in turn setting them free. This is exactly what Jesus did for us. We were guilty of our sin, and our sin deserved to be judged, but He took the punishment on Himself. The theological word for this is *"propitiation"*. It means appeasing or atonement. Jesus did not just ignore our past, He actually paid for it. He atoned for it. He took the penalty of our past sins upon Himself. Colossians 2:13-14 says:

> *"13 You were dead because of your sins and because your sinful nature was not yet cut away. Then God made you alive with Christ, for he forgave all*

*our sins. 14 He cancelled the record of the charges against us and took it away by nailing it to the cross."*

When we realise the debt has been paid in full we don't need to feel guilty about it anymore. The gift of the cross is beautiful and liberating. The song 'Amazing Grace' was written by John Newton, a former slave trader turned pastor and slavery abolitionist, and he wrote about how He "saved a wretch like me...". We were the guilty, but he makes us innocent. We were so broken, we were so in debt to Him, and our sin was so great, but yet His grace covered it altogether. That's why the Grace of God is so amazing. When we fully understand who we are without God we can fully understand His grace towards us. Grace rescued us from the sin we were in. We were so broken, so down and out, and Jesus loved us. Jesus took a hold of our past for us.

The bible states Godly sorrow leads to repentance which leaves no regrets (2 Corinthians 7:10) Now we can look to our past without guilt. Once we have brought it to Jesus He has dealt with it on our behalf. The cross changes your past!

## 2. How does the cross change the way I see my present?

When I was younger my parents would sometimes take me and my older sisters to an amusement park. I always loved roller coasters and as a little kid I longed to ride them, but for many years I was unable to, why? Because I was too short. I would hop in line and just as I was about to get to the front, there would be a man standing next to a sign, usually a cut out image of a clown holding his hand up, and the speech bubble protruding from the clown's head said 'You must be this tall to ride'. Time and time again I would step up and fall short. I didn't live up to the standard required. I think this is how many people feel on the inside, a sense of not quite living up to the standard. The standards that society holds us to, that others hold us to, and even those that we hold ourselves too.

And so, a lot of people in today's society are extremely insecure. It is not a new problem, it's a human problem that's always been there. I want to bring your attention to the word 'righteous' or 'righteousness'. The word righteous by definition means to be pleasing, presentable, and without shame. The desire to be righteous is within each and every one of us. Deep down inside the human condition is the longing to be pleasing, presentable and without shame before someone. But where did this come from? It all started in the beginning. When Adam and Eve disobeyed God and sin entered into the world, they immediately tried to hide their nakedness and shame, so what did they do? They made coverings for themselves with fig leaves (Genesis 3:7) as they were trying to make themselves presentable, pleasing, and without shame, trying to make themselves righteous.

What happens to a leaf once it's plucked from the branch? It stays green for a while but eventually it withers up and dies. So it is with our own versions of righteousness. It seems to work for a while, but eventually it fails. Why? Because we cannot make ourselves truly presentable, pleasing and without shame. Self righteousness is a fragile temporary solution to our desperate need to be made right. We can't do it in our own human effort. If we look to everyone else to validate us, to make us pleasing, for acceptance and love, you are always going to feel insecure. We will always feel fear. The answer to this need is to pour our present through the filter of the cross. We need to understand it's through the cross we now truly see ourselves.

When we see ourselves through the cross we must see what's referred to as "Imputed Righteousness". Imputed means to credit to someone, so imputed righteousness means that Jesus' righteousness has now been credited to us. It's Jesus saying, "I'll give you my righteousness". Jesus lived a perfect life, pleasing, presentable and without shame. He has taken our life and has given us His. Jesus has taken our sin, our shame, our insecurity, our fear and has given us His righteousness. The great exchange! Paul says in 2 Corinthians 5:21:

> *"For our sake he made him to be sin who knew no sin, so that in him we might become the righteousness of God."*

The world says DO the work and get love, identity and security.

The cross says the work is done! Now we RECEIVE, love, identity and security.

The cross changes our heart and mind to realise we are not working to receive love but working from love. We are not working to make ourselves more presentable because Jesus has already made us presentable before God our Father. Understanding this will change the way we live and view our present!

### 3. How does the cross change the way I see my future?

I am a huge movie buff and one of the great movies I've seen is the movie 'Unbroken'. It is based on true story about a US Olympic track record holder, Louis Zamperini, who pulls himself through a plane crash in the Second World War only to be left stranded floating for days in the middle of the ocean. He is caught and caged up in a Japanese prisoner of war camp and eventually gets liberated and saved by the American army. As I watched this movie I was on the edge of my seat, anxious but hopeful that he would pull through. I was so relieved to see him liberated at the end. I enjoyed the movie so much that, not long after, I watched it again. Only this time I knew what would happen, I knew how it ended. This is how Jesus' followers should view our future. We know and expect that life will have its ups and downs, but we should take confidence in this - we know how it ends. Romans 8:38 Paul declares:

> *"And I am convinced that nothing can ever separate us from God's love. Neither death nor life, neither angels nor demons, neither our fears for today nor our worries about tomorrow—not even the powers of hell can separate us from God's love."*

Paul admits there will be opposition, but he is convinced, and we should be too, that NOTHING can separate us from the love of God. Why does that change the way we view our future? If nothing can break or shake up the love of God, it gives us such a great sense of peace for the future. Regardless of what happens, God's love is always going to be there. With God's love comes His power, His provision, His presence so we don't need to worry about our future.

Because of the cross, we have received an unshakeable and unbreakable love. We don't know *what* the future holds but we do know *who* holds the future. So we can look to our future knowing God's unshakeable love will always be there. That gives us a filter to now view our future through. Even though the world may shake around us, His love never will. God's love will never change for us! It's all proven through the work of the cross. The cross shows us that there is nothing that can separate us from God's love because Jesus has made a way for us to access that love.

When we view our lives through the cross we can see our past, present and future through a new lens. The lens of the cross.

## **PAUSE AND REFLECT:**

- ❖ Is there an area of your past you need to take to the cross?
- ❖ Are you trying to DO things to gain acceptance and security in your life? If so, bring them Jesus, allow the gift of his righteousness to drown out those insecurities.
- ❖ How does knowing that God's love is unbreakable change the way you see your future.

## A PRAYER:

*"Father I thank you for sending your Son, Jesus, to die on the cross for me, and Jesus I thank you for willingly laying down your life. Help me to bring my past, present and future to the cross and view it through the cross. Let it change the way I live. Amen.*

CHAPTER 6

# FOUNDATIONS: The Person and Power of the Holy Spirit

*"16 So I say, walk by the Spirit, and you will not gratify the desires of the flesh. 17 For the flesh desires what is contrary to the Spirit, and the Spirit what is contrary to the flesh. They are in conflict with each other, so that you are not to do whatever you want. 18 But if you are led by the Spirit, you are not under the law. 19 The acts of the flesh are obvious: sexual immorality, impurity and debauchery; 20 idolatry and witchcraft; hatred, discord, jealousy, fits of rage, selfish ambition, dissensions, factions 21 and envy; drunkenness, orgies, and the like. I warn you, as I did before, that those who live like this will not inherit the kingdom of God. 22 But the fruit of the Spirit is love, joy, peace, forbearance, kindness, goodness, faithfulness, 23 gentleness and self-control. Against such things there is no law.*

> ²⁴ *Those who belong to Christ Jesus have crucified the flesh with its passions and desires. ²⁵ Since we live by the Spirit, let us keep in step with the Spirit." (Galatians 5:16- 25)*

One of the greatest pop stars of our time was Michael Jackson. He wrote and released so many great hits, but one in particular that has always been a favourite for me was a song released in 1988 called 'Man in the Mirror'. There are two types of people reading this book. The first type doesn't even really know who Michael Jackson is because they were born post-2000. The second type is already singing the chorus to the song in their head:

> *"I'm starting with the man in the mirror*
> *I'm asking him to change his ways*
> *And no message could have been any clearer*
> *If you want to make the world a better place*
> *Take a look at yourself, and then make a change."*

I think this song was such a hit because it spoke to one of our deepest desires, our desire to change. We all know there is something wrong in the world and in us. But how do we right that wrong? How do we make a change? How do *we* change? This is a huge question that has plagued mankind for centuries. And most people have come to the same conclusion as Michael Jackson. If I'm going to make the world a better place, then I've got to start with me. So off we go on the journey of self-help or self-improvement. It's estimated that close to 45,000 self-help books are released each year around the world, and they are selling just as quickly as they are being released. There is nothing inherently wrong with self help but there are two major issues that you will quickly discover:

## 1. Self help is not sustainable

It takes a tremendous amount of personal energy and effort to change yourself. You must consistently work at it and eventually it will leave you physically, mentally and emotionally exhausted. Or you will have to make it a consistent ruse that you must keep up in order to impress others with your new and improved self.

## 2. Self help can change the surface but fails to deal with the deeper issues

Self help can change external actions, it can even have a short term effect on your attitude. But it fails to bring change to the deepest part of you, your heart and your desires.

There is a restlessness within us for change because we are made in the image of God. Our inner desire is to be more like Him. We all want to change, but so often we just don't know how to do it. We get tired trying to keep up with our own desire to change. We work to bring it about by gathering external things we think will bring change, but external things cannot bring true lasting change from the inside out. The power to change is within a divine God. Only the Spirit of God can bring internal, lasting change. True change is out of our control! So what are we to do?

There is a power that God has given us access to. It's not an ethereal power but a person, who wants to be at work in and through our lives to bring change. This is the person and the power of the Holy Spirit.

## Who Is the Holy Spirit?

The Holy Spirit is a distinct member of the triune community of love we call the Trinity. There is so much we could say about the Holy Spirit, but the easiest way I can describe the Holy Spirit is that He is the Spirit of Jesus at work IN YOU and WITH YOU. He is the one who has the ability to know, search, reveal and heal the deepest parts of our broken lives. He nurtures and grows the love of God within us and He is there to teach us and lead us in the ways of Jesus (Psalms 139:1-24, Romans 5:5, Ezekiel 36:27). When you made the decision to put your faith and trust in Jesus, the Holy Spirit entered into your life and His role is to help us change to become more and more like the Jesus version of ourselves as we partner with Him.

It is extremely important that we give attention to the foundation of the person and the power of the Holy Spirit as He is God's gift to help us change.

## How does the Holy Spirit outwork change in our lives?

In every single person there is a war of the worlds on the inside. When we say yes to Jesus a new desire steps in and it wants to live like Him, but there is also an old desire inside of us that wants to live in our old way of life. These desires are constantly at war. This is why God has sent His Holy Spirit. We need to learn to trust the Holy Spirit in our lives (Galatians 5:16-17). He is the power to change. Lasting change doesn't happen because you try harder, lasting change happens because you learn to trust better in the person of the Holy Spirit.

The Apostle Paul is writing to the church in Galatia because they started this journey of trusting in Jesus and allowed the Holy Spirit to change them, but then went back to trying to change themselves. Galatians 3:1-3 says:

> *"You foolish Galatians! Who has bewitched you? Before your very eyes Jesus Christ was clearly portrayed as crucified. ² I would like to learn just one thing from you: Did you receive the Spirit by the works of the law, or by believing what you heard? ³ Are you so foolish? After beginning by means of the Spirit, are you now trying to finish by means of the flesh?"*

Paul is saying change started through the Holy Spirit and it continues through the Holy Spirit. But this is not a one off decision, it's a constant decision we must make. *Once you have said yes to Jesus, transformation is a daily 'spirit-fuelled' choice between your <u>old self</u> and your <u>new self</u>.*

If you make that daily decision to keep partnering with the Holy Spirit there are 3 things the Holy Spirit does within you to bring about change in your life:

## 1. The Holy Spirit brings gradual change

In Galatians 5:22 Pauls writes

> "But the **fruit** of the Spirit is ...."

If I was to take an orange seed and plant it in my backyard and then expect that the next day a huge orange tree would be there, you would call me crazy! Because we all know that it takes time. Sometimes the Holy Spirit does bring about radical instant change in the form of freedom, healing or personal breakthrough. But for the most part our change through the Spirit is gradual. In fact most of the time, the bible refers to spiritual transformation in botanical terms. We are likened to trees that gradually grow and, like a tree, a lot of growth happens below the surface before it's seen above. That does not mean that growth isn't happening. It's just slow and unseen.

We want change to be instant. But all great change happens through a gradual process. In a similar way the Holy Spirit is producing change and growth within us at a gradual pace.

Once I was on holidays with my family and we were driving through a farming region of inland New South Wales. Something caught my attention and I quickly pulled the car over to take a closer look. It was a tree and it looked like it was growing on top of a massive round boulder, but on closer inspection I realised that the tree was in fact not grown on top of the boulder but had grown straight through the middle of it. How could the hard surface of the rock be penetrated by the roots of a tree? It burst through the seemingly impenetrable substance through slow, gradual growth. So it is with the Holy Spirit's growth in you. You may think there are things you could never experience breakthrough in, because they are too hard, but just trust the gradual growth of the Holy Spirit. As you trust the Holy Spirit, He starts to produce the fruit of the Spirit in you.

Galatians 5:22- 23 says:

> *"²² But the fruit of the Spirit is love, joy, peace, forbearance, kindness, goodness, faithfulness, ²³ gentleness and self-control. Against such things there is no law."*

Paul says that if you trust in the gradual change of the Holy Spirit you will start to experience love, joy, peace, forbearance, kindness, etc. He is not saying that you should try to produce these things, but that the Spirit will produce these in you. The fruit is the byproduct, the Spirit is the prime product.

## How do I know if the Holy Spirit is gradually changing me?

The greatest way we can know the Holy Spirit is changing us is when we face pressure, problems and hardship. This is when our change is revealed. As we grow we approach our problems and hardships in a different way than we did before. Where there was hate or indifference there is now a growing love. Where there was despair, there is now expanding joy. Where there was anxiousness and fear there is now increasing peace. This is just some of the evidence of an internal change that the Holy Spirit is doing.

## 2. The Holy Spirit brings internal change

Real change is not an external change, it comes from within. The Amplified bible says it like this in Galatians 5:22:

> *"22 But the fruit of the Spirit is (the result of His presence within us) ..."*

When we receive Jesus, the Holy Spirit now lives within us and begins to change our desires. It is this power within us that brings internal change. Our past is not stronger than the Holy Spirit within us. It is the same power within us that rose Christ from the grave and now lives in us (Romans 8:11). It is an internal change.

There is a difference however between religious external change and Holy Spirit internal change. We can convince ourselves that we have changed, but what we are often looking to is not internal change, it's religious external change. In other words we look at our changed external behaviour:

- I got to church on Sundays
- I have new Christian friends
- I stopped doing some of the things I used to do
- I've started helping others

These are all good things but we must be careful we are not just looking at religious external change without looking at the Holy Spirit's internal change. Just because our environment has changed doesn't mean we have changed. Only the Holy Spirit within us can bring internal change. A.W.Tozer says:

> *"Religion can reform a person's life, but it can never transform him. Only the Holy Spirit can transform!"*

Now you might read that and become paranoid, asking yourself "Am I just experiencing religious external change or real internal Holy Spirit change??" Just relax, take a breath. Assessment is not a bad thing, but let's give our attention to the Holy Spirit and what He can and wants to do in you. Paul says in Galatians 5 the Holy Spirit brings internal change:

- He changes desires (heart)
- He changes thoughts (mind)
- He changes emotions (soul)

Change is a promise. If we are not experiencing internal change we need to pray and invite the Holy Spirit to change us. Simply pray...Come Holy Spirit! And trust Him to change us from the inside out. The fruit of the Spirit will come and will be evident in our lives.

### 3. THE HOLY SPIRIT BRINGS INEVITABLE CHANGE

Inevitable change will happen depending on who you trust. We can say yes to Jesus and yes to the Holy Spirit working in us, but if we are not really trusting in Him we will continue to return to doing things in our own strength and trusting in ourselves to bring change. Inevitable change will happen as we start to trust in the person of the Holy Spirit. In Galatians 5 Paul says two things:

> "¹⁹ The **acts of the flesh** are obvious..... "²² But the **fruit of the Spirit** is..."

Notice the difference. The acts vs the fruit. One I do, the other I receive. One is doing, the other is letting. This is a trust thing. If we keep acting in our flesh, our flesh will continue to fail us. Or we can receive the Holy Spirit and just watch the fruit happen. One is doing, one is receiving. Lasting change doesn't happen because you try harder, lasting change happens because you learn to trust better in the Holy Spirit.

### 4. The Holy Spirit leads to spirit fueled obedience

Obedience has almost become a dirty word in our modern day context, but Jesus said "If you love me you will obey my commandments". To follow Jesus is to let him take the lead, to let him call the shots. The truth is we struggle with this because we love being in control. But the beautiful part of the Holy Spirit's role in our lives is that He slowly helps us take our hand off the wheel of our lives and helps us to trust Jesus and His way. He helps us understand that Jesus is not following us, we are following Jesus.

The Holy Spirit is leading us to obedience. How does He lead us? He leads us in many ways, but one of the main ways the Holy Spirit leads us to obedience is through conviction. What does conviction mean? To convince of truth, to cross examine or correct.

The Holy Spirit helps us determine what are lies and what is truth. The Holy Spirit cross examines our heart and desires to make sure they are healthy and then He corrects. He points out the wrong, the sin that is robbing us of joy and points us back towards abundant life in Jesus.

There is a difference between conviction and condemnation. Condemnation points out your sin and pushes you down and brings you shame. Conviction points out sin, pulls you back to your feet and points you towards the richness of God's mercy and grace. Romans 8:1 says "So now there is no condemnation for those who belong to Christ Jesus". Condemnation is not from God, it's from the enemy of your soul, but conviction is from the Holy Spirit. When condemnation comes knocking, don't open the door, but when conviction does, gladly welcome it.

## **PAUSE AND REFLECT:**

- ❖ Take time to sit and invite the Holy Spirit into this moment. You could simply say the words "Come Holy Spirit" and then just sit and be still.
- ❖ Ask the Holy Spirit if there are any areas you are yet to trust Him with. Open yourself up to His conviction and trust that He is leading you to life.
- ❖ Ask the Holy Spirit to produce the fruit He brings in your life and to help stay in step with Him.

## A PRAYER:

*"I welcome you Holy Spirit. I am tired of trying to change myself, I want you to bring change into my life. Bring deep internal change in my life. Change any thoughts, desires or emotions that are not in alignment with who I am designed to be. Help me to trust you and not to go back to my old ways. Change me. Amen."*

# FORMATION PRELUDE

When I was growing up, one of my favourite things to play with was Play-doh. I would sit there for hours and shape a horse, a dinosaur, a lion. I could shape just about anything. The play-doh was so malleable all it needed was shaping. We as human beings are extremely similar, we are pliable people being shaped by so many things around us. The question isn't 'are we being shaped?', that is inevitable, but rather 'what are we being shaped by most?'. Over these next few chapters we are going to take a journey through some practices that will help form your faith and follow-ship of Jesus in a greater way.

We have spent the last few chapters establishing the foundations of our faith which are extremely important. We never move on from them, we grow deeper into them. The next part of our discipleship journey is the formation of our faith. There are many more things that can and will help shape and form your faith, these are just some that helped generations of disciples become greater followers of Jesus. These things are not just beliefs but practices. The shaping and forming comes not from our observation of these things, but our participation. So let's begin.

CHAPTER 7

# FORMATION:
# Community Accountability

> *"I want you to know how much I have agonised for you and for the church at Laodicea, and for many other believers who have never met me personally. 2 I want them to be encouraged and knit together by strong ties of love. I want them to have complete confidence that they understand God's mysterious plan, which is Christ himself."*
> (Colossians 2:1-2)

It's amazing that in a world that is so interconnected so many people still struggle with loneliness and isolation. The danger of our time is that we are now pursuing community connection through inanimate objects like our phones. We have gone from community to audience. From friendships to followers. From tables to tablets. From lounge room deep and meaningful conversations, to instagram DM chats. We've replaced real, deep relationships with surface level acquaintances. We are not experiencing real and authentic community, and deep down inside we know it. Richard Plass and James Cofield sum it up brilliantly in their book 'The Relational Soul':

> *"Practically every human being has experienced that strange inner gnawing, that mental hunger, that unsettling unrest that makes us say, 'I feel lonely'. Loneliness is one of the most universal experiences....what does loneliness tell us about ourselves? Be it chronic or acute, slight or significant, loneliness is proof of our relational design."*

From the very beginning when God made Adam, Genesis 2:18 says;

> *"It's not good for the man to be alone..."*

We must note that God didn't say it was 'impossible for man to be alone', He just said it was not good. This alludes to the fact we can do it, but the ramifications of a life lived alone aren't just isolation, it's harmful to our wellbeing. Community is not optional, it's vital. Jesus didn't come to build a new religion to fill buildings, Jesus came to build a new community who would share their faith and life together, to become people of love. When it comes to our spiritual formation, community isn't just about good company, community is about good accountability.

Community accountability is about redeeming the need for human connection. We all have a deep need for company and we all know there is a realistic side to loneliness.

We all need meaningful connections that are found only in real, authentic community.

I'm sure you are reading this and, chances are, you agree. You know we need and long for community, but still we struggle to build deep authentic relationships.

## What prevents authentic community?

### Our Culture

We live in a culture that is constantly bombarding us with messages like 'You do you', and 'Follow your dream'. Subconsciously this reinforces you to focus on yourself and now our relationships become more like rungs on a ladder we use to help advance our dream or pursuit of success. Hyper-individualism by definition is 'a tendency for people to act in a highly individual way, without regard to society'. This is the culture we are living in and it rages against authentic community. You weren't saved and invited into a private journey of following Jesus. You were saved and invited into a family of followers who, together, follow Jesus.

### Time Pressure

One of the most frequent replies you will hear when you ask someone how they have been is 'busy'. And most likely it's true. We have filled our lives with so many responsibilities and activities, that we just don't have time for community. Busyness is a firewall to authentic community, it prevents people from entering into the depths of your life. Time is our most precious commodity and wherever you invest your time reveals what you value most. The only way to make community a value is by investing time.

**Fear**

I think this is the greatest reason we don't enter into an authentic community. We are so given to the projection of perfection that we fear what others may think if we invite them behind the curtain of our lives. The truth is, once we push past the fear and enter into vulnerability, we are surprised to discover that we are all very much the same. We all have problems and issues, we are all just human beings facing similar fears, struggles and anxieties. I get it, vulnerability is scary but it's necessary if you want to experience the type of community you long for. It's in that place of vulnerability where fear is drowned out by the love and support of others.

In Colossians Paul sees the danger of living separate from community. The greatest way our relationship with Jesus is going to grow is not only through personal time with God but with intentional community time with others. In Christ-centred community we encourage each other towards growing in Christ. We share the burdens of each other's lives and together, we stir one another on in this journey called life.

The Apostle Paul speaks into the plan for community accountability in Colossians 2:1-2;

> *"1 I want you to know how much I have agonised for you and for the church at Laodicea, and for*

*many other believers who have never met me personally. 2 I want them to be encouraged and knit together by strong ties of love. I want them to have complete confidence that they understand God's mysterious plan, which is Christ himself."*

Paul writes to the church in Colossae and he says I agonise for you. He really wants them to get it. He is imploring them to see what church is really all about. It's not just about growing in personal knowledge of God, it's about joining with others to discover and grow more like Jesus.

God's plan is not that you would just sit together, but that you would be knit together. There is a difference between the two:

**A Sit together church:**

- Enjoys foyer conversations, but no deeper than that.
- Enjoys familiar conversation, but not unfamiliar ones.
- Shows up sporadically on Sundays.
- See's church as a requirement and less of a benefit.

**A Knit together church:**

- Sees the imperative need for consistent community.
- Gives time to Jesus-centred community consistently on Sundays and throughout the week.
- See church as a family they belong to, not just a service they attend
- Joyfully follows Jesus' example in serving others.

Paul's hope for the church in Colossae was that it would be knit together by the strong ties of love, but this is not easy. It requires commitment, energy and effort. A good example of how community accountability works is rock climbing. Each climber is tied to someone in front and someone behind. There is a mountain, rope and a goal to climb the mountain. Our faith journey is like climbing a mountain. We are meant to ascend in our relationship with God. But it's not meant to be done alone. We all need climbing buddies, or someone we are roped to, someone who is ahead of us on our faith journey. We need to be roped to them so they can help and encourage us to go higher in our faith.

I believe we should also intend to have someone roped to us. This is one of the greatest things we can do for our faith. Someone we can help climb the mountain and encourage on their journey of faith. Someone we can share our experience with and help them up the mountain. Through community, we rope ourselves together and climb higher in our faith. We should be roped to someone ahead of us and roped to someone behind us. Using this illustration in the context of Colossians 2:2;

- The rope represents love. We are knit or tied together by the strong ties of love.
- The mountain is the upward journey of transformation
- The goal is understanding and becoming more like Jesus.

This is how we should be attached relationally - roped together, spurring one another on. A few climbing truths to remember:

- We all start at the bottom
  - Everyone starts like a newborn, and grows in their faith - just keep climbing. We all need to learn to climb.
- We won't be an expert straight away
  - We train and condition ourselves to learn how to follow God
  - The greatest way to learn is to be roped to someone. Remember, we all need climbing buddies
- The goal is onwards and upwards
  - We are not meant to stay where we are, we are not meant to stay at base camp.

## What does community accountability look like?

### 1. We commit to one another

1 Thessalonians 2:8 says:

> "8 so we cared for you. Because we loved you so much, we were delighted to share with you not only the gospel of God but **our lives** as well. "

Community is not convenient, it is a commitment. Community needs to become a priority in order for it to be of benefit. When things aren't a priority we make excuses. When things are a priority we make time. We must be committed to each other. Christ-centred community is not just about sharing the Gospel it's about sharing our lives. We need to recognise that this is not a perfect journey, church community is full of imperfections. People say they want an authentic community but it doesn't mean perfect, it means real. Take, for instance, an apple. When you go to an organic fruit store, you'll notice the apples aren't as clean, shiny and symmetrical as the ones in the mainstream store. In fact they are a bit misshapen, have blemishes and imperfections. The reason being is that they haven't been chemically altered, they are organic, they are authentic. So it is with an authentic church community. Imperfections are inevitable, we are pushing past the shiny manufactured veneer and getting into the rawness of each other's lives. Don't see the imperfections as a turn off, they are mostly there to develop and bring the Christ-like nature out of you and cause you to grow. Don't cut the rope on others, but journey through our imperfections together. Commit to community.

**2. We support one another**

Galatians 6:2 says:

> *"Share each other's burdens, and in this way obey the law of Christ."*

Christ centred community is when we share one another's burdens. What burdens them, burdens you and vice versa. When we share one another's burdens it alleviates the weight. The Holy Spirit gives us a supernatural ability to do this. He leads us to humility which leads us to transparency with others. Ultimately the strong ties of love lead us to recognise we are in this together. If we lose our footing we are tied to someone who can keep us going. It's in confessing our burdens and weaknesses that freedom is found. When we share, we understand we are not the only one. Burdens were never meant to be carried alone.

**3. We inspire one another towards living like Jesus.**

Hebrews 10:24-25 says

> *"Let us think of ways to motivate one another to acts of love and good works. And let us not neglect our meeting together, as some people do, but encourage one another."*

It is so important that we get around people that will motivate and spur us on to become more like Jesus. Like coals in a fire, the closer they are together the more fire remains, but remove a coal from the fire, it loses heat and fire quickly. We need each other to keep a fire for Jesus blazing in our hearts and lives. The writer of Hebrews says to think of ways to motivate each other. This is not just the "pastors" job on a Sunday, but a shared responsibility for all believers. Some days you are going to need encouragement and some days you will be the encourager, but don't neglect getting together in church and in groups, we need each other.

**4. We lead one another closer to Jesus.**

Jude1:20 says:

> *"But you, dear friends, must build each other up in your most holy faith."*

Inspiring and leading are two different things. Inspiring is leading by example, whereas to lead is a deeper sense of friendship, relationship and intentional connection. It's where we come alongside each other and encourage one another to go a bit deeper. In our relationship with Jesus we must make the time to come alongside one another.

We also need to recognise the word accountability. In order to make community work best, you must make yourself accountable to others. Here are some of the best ways to establish community accountability:

### Pursue intentional Jesus-focused community

Part of community is just hanging out and enjoying a good meal together. But we must also have intentional Jesus-focused community; a group of people you gather with and unpack scripture, ask questions, and pray for each other. You are intentionally pursuing Jesus together. Most churches have connect groups or small groups, these are incredibly great ways to help you grow in Jesus and in community. Sunday alone won't cover all the bases, Jesus-focused small groups are essential. If you can't find one, start one.

### Establish a consistent confession session

For centuries the church has encouraged people towards the act of confession. It was in the 13th century that the catholic church made this a mandatory annual occasion for every church member to confess their sins to a priest or spiritual leader. However, James 5:16 says:

> *"Confess your sins to each other and pray for each other so that you may be healed."*

The Apostle James is saying that confession is something designed to be consistently practised, not necessarily with a pastor or church leader but with each other! We must establish an honest and vulnerable moment, not with everyone, but with someone we can share our sins with. What you keep in the dark grows, but what you bring into the light loses its grip. In the early parts of my christian journey, I would typically bring my sins to a pastor or leader in my life. It was only a few years ago that I intentionally set aside a weekly or fortnightly meeting with a very close Christian friend with the intention of confession. We call it our *'confession session'*. We typically sit in a cafe and bring into the light the sins we knowingly feel are hidden in our hearts. It's awkward and semi embarrassing at first, but I cannot explain the freedom and joy it produces in us once we have confessed our sins. On top of that, it has taken the depth of our relationship from friend to brother and has strengthened our character in Jesus.

### GIVE SOMEONE PERMISSION TO WOUND YOU

Proverbs 27:6 says:

> *"Wounds from a friend can be trusted, but an enemy multiplies kisses."*

King Solomon is saying that people who only tell you what you want to hear are actually an enemy to your growth and development, but a friend will wound you with truth if they need to. In my opinion this actually works best when you give people permission to wound you. Give them licence to point out your blind spots, because we all have them. Healthy church community does this because we love each other. The reason we don't often tell the truth to each other is because we would rather preserve the relationship than help the individual. This is not love, it's selfishness. We must speak the truth in love from a place of love and we must give people permission to do so. Someone posted a question on instagram recently that said;

"If someone was new to following Jesus, what would be the first thing you would teach them?"

My immediate response: "Community Accountability."

When Jesus called the disciples to follow Him, He didn't just call them to Himself, He called them to the community. A majority of spiritual formation and growth is going to take place in the context of community. Make sure you find it and commit to it.

## **PAUSE AND REFLECT:**

- ❖ Who have you placed around you that is encouraging you to be more like Jesus?
- ❖ Who can you be roped to that is ahead of you in your faith?

- ❖ Who is someone that you are ahead of in the faith journey that could be roped to you and help with their faith journey?
- ❖ Confession is a huge part of your freedom and growth, who can you establish a confession session with?

## A PRAYER:

*"Jesus I thank you for the gift that is the church. That you placed me in a family who would help me to follow and grow in my faith. Help me to be brave enough to go deeper in community, to open up my life and invite others in. Give me strength to do this. Amen."*

CHAPTER 8

# FORMATION: Reflective Reading

*"10 Put on your new nature, and be renewed as you learn to know your Creator and become like him." (Colossians 3:1-10 NLT)*

I used to watch a show with my kids called 'American Pickers'. The show follows two antique and collectable experts around the US as they try to buy various items for resale, clients, or for their personal collections. I know it doesn't sound that riveting but it is actually really entertaining. It's especially interesting when they go into the backyard of some 87 year old hoarder's barn and beneath the boxes and junk they see a large object hidden amongst the mess. They pull away the junk and they see a rusty old shell of a car. They gasp and quickly make an offer because they know this car is a classic and, when properly reconstructed and refurbished, it would be worth a lot. They know what it was meant to be and what it could be.

This is what the word of God has the capability to produce in you. God knows who you are meant to be and what you could be, His word leads you to a place where, through the power of His truth, you could be reconstructed and into who he designed you to be all along. On top of that, His word does not just reveal your original design, but the grand designer, God himself. This is what God's word has the power to do.

Paul writes to the church in Colossae and says that we have a new nature, God is putting new desires in us but then he uses the word *'renewed'*. The Greek word is *anakainoó* which means *'to make new again'*. Another translation says *'God's ever-transforming journey of a believer'*. God is always trying to bring us back to the original state He designed, fashioned and formed us to live in. The word 'know' in the Greek is *ginóskó* which means 'personally, intimately, and experientially know something'. In this verse "know" refers to our foundations (The Father Heart of God) and "become" refers to our continued transformation. In other words, 'knowing leads to becoming'. It is through scripture that we discover God and ourselves in a greater way.

## What is the bible?

The word bible in Greek is *'Biblos'* which means 'The book', in Latin it's *'Ta bibli'* which means 'the books'. Basically, the word bible means a library of books. In fact it's made up of 66 books; 39 in the old testament, also known as the *'Tanakh'*. Jews saw the Tanakh as a compilation of books and different styles of writing, starting with the first five books, (Genesis to Deutoronomy) which focuses on Israel's story and God's laws. The other parts of the old testament were made up of prophecy about God's ultimate plan for His people and poetic writings. The New

Testament begins with the Gospels, which are the disciples' eyewitness accounts of Jesus, His life, and His teachings. Then, there is the Book of Acts, which documents roughly the first 30 years of the New Testament church and the Apostles' writings to various churches all around the known world. All together, these writings weren't just a manual for human living but also a story about God and His desire to be in a relationship with His creation.

The bible is a library that tells a story that leads to an invitation.

### What is the overall story of the bible?

Timothy Keller says:

> "The Bible is the grand narrative of God's relationship with humanity, a story of grace, redemption, and ultimate hope...."The Bible is not a series of disconnected events; it's a coherent and epic story of creation, fall, redemption, and restoration."

The NIV bible tells this story in 728,000 words. Here is the extremely condensed version in less than 500:

An all-powerful being called God creates the world. In His love, God makes mankind in His own image to rule, reign, and co-create this new world with Him. He gives mankind the choice of trusting Him, to build this new world together and to let God define what is good and evil, or they could take power and define good and evil on their own.

They are tempted by a dark, deceptive and mysterious creature who suggests they should decide good and evil for themselves. They choose to trust in themselves, leading humanity into despair and causing a great rift between mankind and God. However, God, who loves humanity, desires to make it right. He begins by creating a new people who will exemplify His character and care for humanity. They will bring goodness and blessings to the world.

God selects an older couple, Abraham and Sarah, to start this new nation of people. They fulfil this purpose, and this nation is eventually called the people of Israel. Yet, even God's chosen people repeatedly choose not to trust Him and instead trust themselves. Humanity persists in wanting to define good and evil independently and go their own way. So God creates laws and ways to make it right. The laws do great things to help create a framework around what humanity should look like, but man's heart is still corrupt and keeps turning towards sin.

Over hundreds of years, the people of Israel cycle through following God's ways, turning away and then choosing their own path. This cycle involves God protecting and caring for them, and them subsequently straying, encountering trouble, and God repeatedly rescuing them. However, God consistently speaks through a group of people called the prophets that someday He will rectify the situation by sending a Messiah—a chosen saviour king who will rescue His people, conquer their greatest enemy, and bring peace and blessings to the world.

At the appointed time, God puts on flesh. Jesus arrives to set things right. His message is to repent and trust Him, as He establishes a new kingdom. Jesus doesn't merely tell them; He shows them, and demonstrates what humanity was always meant to look like. He heals, brings love and justice, and reveals God's heart to the world. Then, He dies on a cross to atone for the sins and shame caused by mankind, starting with Adam and Eve, and extending to all future sins. In doing so, He restores the severed connection with God that began in the garden with Adam and Eve.

After rising from the dead, Jesus tells His followers to continue His work, inviting others to join a new community of faith, hope, and love. This community will help others connect with God through Jesus. Although Jesus ascends to heaven, He doesn't abandon His followers. He sends the Holy Spirit to dwell within them. While in the garden, God walked and talked with Adam and Eve, but now the Holy Spirit resides within the hearts of all believers, walking and talking with them every day. The Holy Spirit also gives them the power to do what mankind struggled with before, He creates in them a heart that longs to trust and obey God. But the story isn't finished. We are now invited to join in God's new plan—to not just cultivate a garden, but to expand a kingdom and create a new family of Jesus' followers. This new family is no longer called Israel; it is called the ecclesia or the church.

FORMATION: REFLECTIVE READING

## What invitation does the bible give us?

N.T. Wright says:

> "The Bible is not just a record of the past; it's a story that invites us to become part of God's ongoing work in the world."

While we can't add to the written text of the bible, we are continuing the story of the bible. We are now a part of God's story or God's plan to reunite humanity with Him and join with Him in creating a new world, a world full of God's love, joy and peace.

## How should we read and apply scripture?

D.L. Moody says:

> "The bible was not given for our information, but for our transformation."

Our lives are just like clay, easily shaped and formed. The only question is, who or what have you allowed to shape or form it? We are continually experiencing moments that shape and form us. They can be positive and they can be negative. Moments like personal achievements, our upbringing, tragic events, regrets and missed opportunities, and personal choices all play a role in shaping us. Sometimes these moments aren't our choice, they are other people's actions. Our lives are very easily shaped, both for good and for bad.

Regardless of how your life has been shaped, there is no life that God can't transform. The world can shape you, but only God can transform you. We must put ourselves into the hand of God like clay on a potter's wheel and allow him to re-shape our lives. He can transform us into the person He desired us to be and the person that deep down we long to be.

When we said yes to Jesus and entrusted our lives over to Him, we received the transformative power of the Holy Spirit, but there are some things we need to do. There are things we need to go to work on. Our faith causes us to do this, not out of demand but out of a desire to change. One of the greatest ways God transforms your life is through his Word. Through reflective reading of the Bible.

Paul writes in 2 Timothy 3:16-17:

> *"16 All Scripture is inspired by God and is useful to teach us what is true and to make us realise what is wrong in our lives. It corrects us when we are wrong and teaches us to do what is right. 17 God uses it to prepare and equip his people to do every good work."*

There are a few things Paul wants Timothy (and us) to know about the word of God:

### 1. Scripture is from God

"16 All Scripture is inspired by God (God Breathed)."

The Bible is not just about God, it is *from* God. It is a letter written from Him to us so we can come to know Him more. This tells us that the Word of God is:

a) God Revealing - You can never truly know someone until you talk to them. We can say we "know" a famous person but until we speak to them we never truly know them. We only know about them. When God speaks to us through His word it reveals who God is. We no longer speculate but we know who God is when we read His word.

b) Life Giving - all scripture is God breathed. When God made Adam from the dust in the book of Genesis, it says He breathed into him and his life started (Genesis 2:7). The same breath that God breathed life into Adam is the same as His Word. It is God breathed and life giving. Scripture brings life.

When you read the Bible you KNOW God and you RECEIVE life.

## 2. Scripture Reveals Right and Wrong

> *"16 All Scripture is inspired by God and is useful to teach us what is true and to make us realise what is wrong in our lives."*

We live in a world that is seeking truth. The only issue is, it's usually a truth that suits them. We look for sources to back up our belief system or our desires. This is why we need the Bible. The

Bible reveals to us what is true and what is false. It is like a mirror that reveals what is right or wrong in our own lives.

Why do we look in a mirror? We look at a mirror when we are getting ready for the day because we want to actually correct and adjust how we appear. It's not just for vanity, it's actually to see what needs to be adjusted. In the same way the Bible corrects and adjusts us. Every day we need to look into the mirror of the Bible so we can adjust the inside. Adjust our thoughts, motives, heart and feelings.

We are all looking for truth, but we must remember, It's not *a truth* that sets you free, it is *the truth* that sets you free. When you read the Bible, it reveals a truth that brings liberty. The only way to know what is right and wrong is to go to the Word of God. He wants to reveal what is wrong in us not to condemn us, but to free us.

### 3. Scripture Corrects and Directs

> *"16 ...It corrects us when we are wrong and teaches us to do what is right.*

When we go against God's word it hurts us, not God. It is important for us to read and take notice of the instruction in the Bible because it is good for us. It corrects and directs us for our protection and for our joy. When you read the bible it's like going to the chiropractor and a coach at the same time.

When you go to the chiropractor it is to readjust what is out of alignment, what is causing us pain. The word of God corrects us to bring us back into alignment with who we are designed, formed and fashioned to be. At times it doesn't feel good, just like when a chiropractor adjusts us, but we know it is beneficial for us. Those moments of pain are there to bring relief, not more pain.

The Bible also coaches. It teaches us how to live in the abundant life Jesus promised. It gives directions on how to enjoy every facet of life including friendships, work, and every kind of relationship. It also shows us how to navigate pain and suffering, how to endure and grow. It provides direction for every area of our life. The Bible corrects and directs us.

## 4. Scripture Prepares and Equips

> *"17 God uses it to prepare and equip his people to do every good work."*

Prepare means to get ready. Equip means to provide and resource. If we were preparing for war we would need to not only be prepared with a strategy for battle, but also be equipped with every resource to fight the battle. Every time you read the bible it gets you ready and equips you for life and ministry. It prepares us by showing examples of how to journey through life, and equips us by showing us how to handle every life situation that comes our way.

So many of us are not prepared or equipped for life because we do not go to the Bible. God has good works He wants to do through us but we need to be prepared and equipped to walk into them. We need to fall in love with the Bible because it's one of the greatest tools God has given us for transformation. We don't just need shaping, we need transforming through reflective reading of the Word.

### How can I read scripture in an applicable way?

I have been around church for many years and this is one of the most common areas people seem to struggle with. There are so many different ways to read scripture, but I would like to point out one that has been impactful for many believers over the centuries. It's a latin term known as *'Lectio Divina'*. *'Lectio' means read* and *'Divina' means* divine, together it means *"divine reading"* and describes a way of reading the Scriptures where we gradually let go of our own agenda and open ourselves to what God wants to say to us.

There have been ways to enter into divine reading, but here is the most common. It was a four part journey of embracing scripture.

**Lectio** - Read it
**Meditatio** - Reflect (Meditate)
**Oratio** - Respond
**Contemplatio** - Rest

## FORMATION: REFLECTIVE READING

### 1. 'Lectio' - Read it

Get a small portion of scripture and read through it 3-4 times, eg; Psalms 23:1-6:

> *"1 The Lord is my shepherd; I have all that I need. 2 He lets me rest in green meadows;he leads me beside peaceful streams. 3 He renews my strength. He guides me along right paths,bringing honour to his name 4 Even when I walk through the darkest valley,I will not be afraid,for you are close beside me. Your rod and your staff protect and comfort me. 5 You prepare a feast for me in the presence of my enemies.You honour me by anointing my head with oil. My cup overflows with blessings. 6 Surely your goodness and unfailing love will pursue me all the days of my life, and I will live in the house of the Lord forever."*

Part of reflective reading is not just reading it once, it's repeatedly reading it. It's like chewing food. The more we chew it, the more the flavour comes out. So when we read over scripture repeatedly we are bringing out the most it has to offer. The scripture will start to fill our minds.

### 2. 'Meditatio' - Reflect or meditate on it

Once you have read the scripture, allow some time to reflect on the scripture. Reflection simply means fixing our thoughts on something - giving it careful consideration. Reflection also means to meditate. There are two types of meditation in this world, worldly and Christian. Worldly meditation is emptying your mind, whereas Christian meditation is filling your mind. The bible says we are to be transformed by the renewing of our minds (Romans 12:2). We are not transformed by the emptying of our minds, but filling our mind with thoughts of God. Your life is heading in the direction of your strongest thoughts. So make Godly thoughts your goal. We can take practical steps to meditate on scripture by doing the following:

- List everything the scripture says about God
- List anything the scripture says about us.

Most people will read scripture to find themselves in it, which is a part of it, but the focus of scripture first and foremost is to point us to God. The Bible reveals Him, His nature and His character. So listing what it says about God helps us to know who He is. From there it leads us to view ourselves in light of God's love, grace, forgiveness, provision, and purpose. Take a moment to ask what this scripture says about God and then take a moment to ask what it says about you.

## 3. Respond to it

Responding is often missed in Bible-reading by believers. To respond is to ask where I need to be obedient. Obedience is not a popular word in modern society but the thing is, everyone is obeying something. Or, the bible goes as far to say everyone is a slave to something. 2 Peter 2:19 says we are slaves to whatever we obey. What are you obeying the most? Scripture calls us to a place of obedience. The bible is not just about attaining intellectual knowledge, it's meant to lead us to Holy Spirit-fuelled trust and obedience.

True, deep transformation happens not through simply knowing scripture but obeying scripture. Not just reading, but putting it into action and applying it to our lives.

Luke 11:28 says *"...Blessed rather are those who hear the word of God and obey it."*

One of the greatest goals of reading the Bible is to *obey*. This is where the blessing and freedom comes. We can take practical steps to obey by listing the following when we read scripture:

- What *examples* need to be followed?
- What *commands* need be to obeyed?
- What things that need to be *avoided*?

All of these things start to help us find transformation through the word of God. It's not just in reading, but in obeying. It's not just about information, it's about transformation.

## 4. Rest in it

This is the part in reflective reading where you sit and be still with God. Rest in the new realities you have just learnt. As Psalm 46:10 says:

> *"Be still, and know that I am God"*

Don't pray, don't meditate, just sit and be still. This isn't an easy thing to do, we are so given to the busy, frantic pace of the world around us, but there is so much peace found in the moments where we just rest in God. As author Ruth Haley Barton writes:

> *"Stillness is the soul's sanctuary where we encounter God's presence and receive His wisdom."*

I want to challenge you. For the next seven days, take up a reflective reading challenge. Choose one scripture and read it repeatedly for seven days, practising the practical steps provided above. Watch what God will reveal to you. This is where transformation starts to happen.

## **PAUSE AND REFLECT:**

- ❖ Open your bible to Psalm 23.
- ❖ If scripture reveals God, what do you think this scripture reveals about God's character and nature?
- ❖ Take time to go through the process of Lectio Devina.
- ❖ Do this for 7 days in a row using this same scripture every time.
- ❖ Write down the different things that God reveals to you through His word.

## **A PRAYER:**

*"God I thank you for giving me your word, I know you intend for it to reveal who you are. Show me who you are in greater ways. Give me a greater passion for your truth. I want to know you more. Amen."*

CHAPTER 9

# FORMATION: Persistent Prayer

> *"Once Jesus was in a certain place praying. As He finished, one of His disciples came to Him and said, "Lord, teach us to pray, just as John taught his disciples." 2 Jesus said, "This is how you should pray: "Father, may your name be kept holy. May your Kingdom come soon. 3 Give us each day the food we need, 4 and forgive us our sins, as we forgive those who sin against us. And don't let us yield to temptation."* (Luke 11:1-4)

What are you really good at? Have you ever heard anyone say, I am really good at prayer? What is it about prayer that is so hard?

When we think of prayer, the truth is it feels:

- boring
- hard work
    - "I can't concentrate"
    - "I don't have the discipline"

- Like God is hard to talk to.
- Like I don't know how to do it.
- Like I don't have time to do it.

We have all these things that run through our minds when it comes to prayer. Most of us feel like we are not good at prayer. We want to get good at it because we are followers of Jesus and we want to follow His example. It was obvious to see Jesus was really good at prayer, in fact he enjoyed it and depended on it! He was fully God, but He was fully man, and in His humanity He recognised that there is a beautiful power, humility and privilege to be able to talk with His Heavenly Father.

In Luke, we see that Jesus' disciples recognise a pattern in Jesus' life. He is regularly taking Himself away to pray. The disciples recognise a correlation between Jesus' prayer life and His ability to live the life He is living, to perform the miracles He is performing, to love the way He is loving.

The disciples are with Jesus all the time and of all the things they could have asked him about, they asked Him "How should we pray?" They asked Jesus about His persistent prayer life. They asked how He did it because they wanted to do the same. They recognised something powerful about prayer and Jesus' prayer life.

As Jesus followers we need to recognise that persistent prayer is one of the most powerful tools we have in our lives.

# FORMATION: PERSISTENT PRAYER

Richard Foster, in his book 'The Celebration Of Discipline' says:

> *'In prayer, real prayer, we begin to think God's thoughts after Him: To desire the things He desires, to love the things He loves, to will the things He wills. Progressively we are taught to see things from His point of view.'*

18th century preacher, Charles Spurgeon says:

> "True prayer is neither a mere mental exercise nor a vocal performance. It is far deeper than that - it is a spiritual transaction with the Creator of Heaven and Earth."

Catholic nun and missionary, Mother Teresa says:

> *"Prayer is putting oneself in the hands of God, at His disposition, and listening to His voice in the depth of our hearts."*

Prayer is so much more than just throwing words or thoughts out into the air. It's about connecting with your Heavenly Father, who also happens to be all loving, all knowing and all powerful.

How do I create a lifestyle of persistent prayer?

## 1. Find your place - Prepare a place and prepare yourself

You can pray anywhere, any time but it is important to carve out a time and a place where you connect daily with your Heavenly Father. Jesus had a prayer place He went to often. It was a place where Jesus knew He could connect with God best.

*Luke 5:16* says:

> *"But Jesus often withdrew to lonely places and prayed."*

Your prayer place needs to be somewhere that is:

- distraction free - don't take your phone with you.
- a place to be present - push out distraction.
- a place to be alone with God - press into a relationship with Him.

## 2. Connect with your Heavenly Father

When Jesus prayed in Matthew 6:9 He said:

> *"Our Father in heaven, may your name be kept holy."*

There are two things we need understand about God:

**He is everywhere** - When we think of our Father in Heaven, we think distance, but the actual term in the Greek was *'ouranos'* meaning "in the air". When Jesus prayed 'our Father in Heaven' he was saying 'Our Father in air.' Air isn't far away, air is everywhere, including inside you. You cannot escape the presence of air. In the same way God cannot be absent! He is present everywhere! He is our ever present Father.

David the Psalmist, says in Psalm 139:7:

> *Where can I go from your Spirit?*
> *Where can I flee from your presence?*

David is speaking of the inescapable presence of God, and he is not speaking it from a place of fear, but of awe and wonder.

St Augustine says:

> *"God is the reality whose centre is everywhere and whose circumference is nowhere."*

So when you pray, remind yourself of the intentional closeness and proximity God has to you. He is not far off, He is incredibly near and present with you.

**He is holy** - Holy means unique, special and without parallel. God is so different. He is not our idea of a father, in fact even the greatest fathers fail in comparison to your heavenly Father. There is no one like Him. He is holy. The most mind blowing part is sin and holiness cannot co-exist. So God in His love, made us Holy through Jesus work on the cross, so we can enjoy the company of our Heavenly Father.

## 3. Ask your father in Heaven

Our prayer life can become a little tainted at times. It is easy to think:

- What will happen will happen
- God's going to do what He wants anyway
- Everything happens for a reason

This approach can sabotage what your prayer life can be. But what if our prayers can change reality? As Christian philosopher and author, Dallas Willard, puts it:

> *"God's response to our prayers is not a charade. He does not pretend that He is answering our prayer when He is only doing what He was going to do anyway. Our requests really do make a difference in what God does or does not do. The idea that everything would happen exactly as it does regardless of whether we pray or not is a spectre that haunts the minds of many who sincerely profess belief in God. It makes prayer psychologically impossible, replacing it with dead rituals at best."*

In other words when you pray some things happen, when you don't pray some things don't happen.

**Your prayers make a difference.**

So when you pray, ask:

- For the kingdom of God in your life and your sphere of life (Your kingdom come)
- For provision (daily bread)
- For forgiveness (forgive me of my sins, and strength to forgive others)
- For strength (don't let us yield to temptation)

Persistent prayer is about us connecting with our Heavenly Father. Our Father in the air, who is everywhere. When we come to Him, we can come with confidence because He is our loving Father. We can connect with Him and ask Him to help us, so pray some bold prayers!

Remember, persistent prayer is talking and connecting with your Heavenly Father, who also happens to be all loving, all knowing and all powerful.

## **PAUSE AND REFLECT:**

- ❖ Take some time in the morning before your day begins, maybe start with 15 minutes. Sit, clear your mind and get your thoughts fixed on God. Imagine Him sitting with you, waiting to spend time with you and hear from you.
- ❖ How do you feel when you connect with God? How does it affect your day?

❖ What are some things you would like to ask God about or for? Write them down and pray over them in your prayer time.

## A PRAYER:

*"Our Father in heaven, hallowed be your name, your kingdom come, your will be done, on earth as it is in heaven. Give us today our daily bread. And forgive us our debts, as we also have forgiven our debtors. And lead us not into temptation, but deliver us from the evil one.*

# CHAPTER 10

# FORMATION: Total Stewardship

*"The earth is the Lord's, and everything in it. The world and all its people belong to Him." Psalm 24:1*

What are the most important priorities in your life? We all have different priorities, but we all have similar ones too. As we mature we begin to share four common areas in our world:

- Our time
- Our talents/gifting
- Our treasure
- Our relationships (family, friends, etc)

Each of these things have worries attached to them and the things we prioritise are generally the things we worry about the most. This is usually because we don't know how to handle them.

What happens when you neglect, mishandle or are ruled by your life priorities? There are some tell tale signs.

## TIME:

When you *neglect* your time, you are *unproductive*.
When you *mishandle* time, you *never have enough*.
When you are *ruled* by time, you are always *too busy*.

## TALENT (GIFTING):

When you *neglect* your talents, you *under-achieve*.
When you *mishandle* your talent, you *waste your potential*.
When you are *ruled* by your talent, you get *arrogant* and are eventually ruled by *selfish ambition*.

## TREASURE (MONEY):

When you *neglect* your money, you get into *debt*.
When you *mishandle* your money, you get *stressed*.
When you are *ruled* by your money, you get *greed*.

## RELATIONSHIPS:

When you *neglect* your relationships, you get *loneliness and isolation*.
When you *mishandle* your relationships, you get *tension and arguments*.
When you are *ruled* by your relationships, you become a *people pleaser*.

So what do we do?

## FORMATION: TOTAL STEWARDSHIP

In Matthew chapter 6:31-33 Jesus addresses the worries of our world.

> *"So don't worry about these things, saying, 'What will we eat? What will we drink? What will we wear?' 32 These things dominate the thoughts of unbelievers, but your heavenly Father already knows all your needs. 33 Seek the Kingdom of God above all else, and live righteously, and he will give you everything you need."*

Jesus tells us to seek first the Kingdom of Heaven. He knows a better way to handle our priorities. He tells us all of these things are good, but when God is not first they are out of order. Worry, anxiety and stress follows when God is not first in our lives. You see, what you worry about is a great revealer of what you worship or what you give worth too. When you worship God and put Him first, worry is made redundant. We trust and rest in God's love and providence. When we order our lives with God first it brings peace, and we begin to steward our time, talent, treasure and relationships well, as God intended.

*Total stewardship is recognising that everything I have is from God, belongs to God, and is not greater than God*

## What does total stewardship look like in your life?

### 1. Your TIME - spend the first part of your day with God.

There is something powerful about putting God first in your day. Before we turn on our phone, prioritise spending time with God. We seek Him first which brings an inner peace to the rest of our day. The gospel of Mark gives us a great example of how Jesus handled it.

*Mark 1:35 says:*

> *"Before daybreak the next morning, Jesus got up and went out to an isolated place to pray."*

Jesus was never in a hurry. He lived and operated in an amazing rhythm of life. He used His time wisely, spending the first of his time with His heavenly Father. Each morning He would go to an isolated place to be alone with God. God also leads us to work and rest well. This is the importance of the Sabbath. One of the greatest acts of worship and faith you can do is take a whole day off. This is a gift for you! When we Sabbath we are trusting God to do what we can't do. Take time to ensure you rest and enjoy. (We will cover the topic of sabbath more in the next chapter.)

### 2. Your TALENTS - let the dominant motive be glorifying Him

When we have total stewardship in our gifts and talents, first and foremost we seek a confident humility. We recognise God has given us talents and abilities and we recognise where it comes from. They are all gifts from God and we use them to glorify Him. Our motive is not selfish ambition but wanting to glorify God. We put God first and our posture is humble yet confident. To steward your giftings is to consistently come before God and ask Him to weigh or search your motives (Proverbs 16:2). God doesn't want you to glorify him with your gifts because He is some narcissistic deity in the sky, absolutely not. God knows that glory or fame is not good for the human heart. We can only handle it in small doses. But when we glorify Him first and humbly recognise the gifts we have are from Him, He is glorified and we are satisfied.

## 3. Your TREASURE - use the first of your money in generosity (tithing & giving)

The first indicator that we are ruled by money is that we can't give it away. When we are not putting God first in this area we want to hold onto our money and we don't trust God with it. We end up being ruled by greed. Greed is a slow releasing poison that corrupts the human heart and causes it to further turn in on itself. This is why we need to ensure we aren't trusting money above God. We need to put Him first above our money and pursue a healthy disregard for money or wealth. The Holy Spirit will help us to manage our money in such a way that we will walk knowing that God will meet our every need and lead us to be generous in every way. Tithing and generosity towards others reminds us that our money is not first, God is. Money is not our provider, God is.

**4. Your RELATIONSHIPS - Make the first goal in your relationships to serve the person.**

We have been conditioned to see relationships as a means to serve ourselves. For example, we see friendship as a means to serve our loneliness, or romantic relationships as a means to serve our need for intimacy. If we are honest, a large part of our desire for people is self serving. So the question we must ask is, How did Jesus handle His relationships? He made the first goal of His relationships to serve people. He came to 'serve and not to be served'. Serving is looking to serve the needs of others. That is what God is asking us to do first and foremost. How can I serve my wife, husband, friends, church, workplace? To steward our relationships is to make serving others the first goal in relationships, not the last.

In summary, total stewardship is recognising that everything I have is from God, belongs to God, and is not greater than God, to ask God how he wants us to handle these important areas of our lives.

## PAUSE AND REFLECT:

- ❖ Consider the 4 priorities of time, talent, treasure and relationships. How well do you manage each of these? Is God first in any or all of these areas?
- ❖ How well are you managing your time? Do you always feel busy and stretched for time?
- ❖ What are some of the gifts and talents God has given you? How are you using them to glorify God?

- ❖ Are you putting God first in the area of money? Do you tithe regularly? If not, why not? Ask God to bring greater understanding and trust with your money.
- ❖ How are your relationships with others? How can you serve others in your relationships?

## A PRAYER:

*"Father, everything I have is from you and is not greater than you. I want to handle all these areas of my life the way you intended. Help me to trust you with my time, my talents, my treasure and my relationships. I trust you Lord. Amen."*

# CHAPTER 11

# FORMATION: Sabbath

We all love the idea of resting, but how often do we truly rest? Even when we do stop, we are often still working on the inside or are heavily distracted by our phone or by the no stop pace of our overly full lives, which in turn makes us restless on the inside. Author and spiritual director Ruth Haley Barton says:

> *"When we keep pushing forward without taking adequate time for rest and replenishment, our way of life may seem heroic, but there is a frenetic quality to our work that lacks true effectiveness because we have lost the ability to be present to God, to be present to other people and to discern what is really needed in our situation."*

So how do we find rest? The Genesis account of creation lets us in on a remarkable observation, God created the world in six days and on the seventh day, the bible says he STOPPED and RESTED (Genesis 2:2-3). God does not get tired or weary, so why did He need to stop? God was giving us a pattern to live by. We are made to work, but we are also meant to stop and rest.

This is why the formation practice of Sabbath is so important. The Hebrew word for sabbath is the world 'Shabbat' which means to 'stop' and 'delight'. Sabbath is actually following God's example of taking time to stop and delight. Immediately we think, surely I don't have time to stop, I have too much to do. But what we need to understand is that God did not design us to go 24/7, and if we do we will feel the effects in our physical, mental, and emotional wellbeing. God's answer to an exhausted world wasn't sporadic moments of escape but a weekly rhythm of rest. Jesus said in Mark 2:27:

> *"The Sabbath was made to meet the needs of people".*

We *need* to sabbath and if you don't find a sabbath, a sabbath will find you. Your body will eventually give in, in the form of break down, burnout or sickness. Sabbath is essential. Peter Scazzero in his book Emotionally Healthy Discipleship says:

> *"We stop and rest on sabbath for a twenty-four-hour period because God is on the throne, assuring us the world will not fall apart if we stop working. God is taking care of the universe and manages quite well without us having to run things."*

Timothy Keller says:

> "The Sabbath is a weekly reminder that we are not slaves to our work, but free and loved children of God."

I love that. Sabbath is one of the greatest acts of faith. It's you shutting down any productivity for a day and trusting that God our heavenly father is still working on your behalf. If Jesus sabbaths then so should we. Everyone should include a day of sabbath in their week to stop and delight. But how?

- **Find a day that works for you**
  - This can vary based on your stage of life, with kids, job demands, etc. But I encourage you to find a day in your week to make a 24 hour period, from sunset one day to sunset the next day. (Note: you may have a few trial and errors in finding a day, but don't give up, this discipline will radically change your life.)
- **Stop (or switch off)**
  - The key to really resting is to switch off. Most of the time this may be literally switching off devices that are causing you to think about work or distract you from being present in the moment. Every other day of the week you are aiming to be productive, but on the sabbath, the goal is not to be productive at all. Stop and rest.

- **Delight**
  - The sabbath isn't just about resting, it's also about delighting or enjoying. Sometimes we are so quick to think about the next week or next thing, but one of the greatest things to do is to reflect on the week you just had and look for moments to be grateful for. Spend a moment on your sabbath to thank God. Cultivate an attitude of gratitude in your life.

Sabbath is not a demand, but a gift. It's establishing a day of rest so that we experience a more sustainable healthy rhythm in our lives.

## PAUSE AND REFLECT:

- ❖ What day would work for you to engage in Sabbath in your seven day week?
- ❖ Create a list to say 'no' to on your Sabbath day. Remove the things that keep your mind engaged on work.
- ❖ When you sabbath, take a few moments to stop and thank God for the things He has given you, the things you are grateful for.

## PRAY:

*"Father, I thank you for the gift of sabbath. I know it will be hard for me to switch off, so help me to rest. Help me to create a healthy rhythm of work and rest in my life. Amen."*

# CONTINUING PRELUDE

The foundation and formation of your faith is extremely important. You never truly move on from them, you just go deeper in your foundation and become more refined in your formation, but it doesn't stop there. Once you say yes to following Jesus you aren't just joining a belief system you are joining a mission to reach the world for the cause of Christ. A disciple is an apprentice and an apprentice is not learning the knowledge of the trade for knowledge's sake, they are learning so they too can do the trade. Jesus' primary goal for His disciples was that they too would have a deep abiding relationship with God, but He also wanted them to go and continue the work that He started. To seek and save the lost, to bring heaven to earth, to heal the sick, serve the poor, bring war to the kingdom of darkness and much more. The 'continuing' stage of the discipleship journey does a few things to you:

1. It prevents you from getting too introspective in your faith and will cause you to look out in order to serve, help and heal the world God loves.
2. It will prevent you from getting bored in your faith. Many believers have become sunday-centric in their

faith, and have made it about sitting in church services, this alone can become very boring, and will inevitably make your faith stagnant.
3. It will pour fuel on the fire of your faith. When you start continuing the work of Jesus, your faith increases in joy and passion as you start to see God move through you as you step out in faith.

The book of Acts is aptly named. One of its original titles was 'The Acts of the Holy Spirit'. You could also say 'The Acts of the Holy Spirit through Jesus followers'. When you read the book of Acts you don't just see a bunch of believers gathered, learning and growing in their faith, you also see the believers scattered throughout the known world sharing their faith and operating in the power of the spirit. This is what it means to continue the ministry of Jesus as one of his disciples.

# CHAPTER 12

## CONTINUING: THE KINGDOM OF HEAVEN

*"Jesus sent out the twelve apostles with these instructions... ⁷ Go and announce to them that the **Kingdom of Heaven** is near." (Matthew 10:5-8)*

If you were to ask people what Jesus talked about the most, most people would say maybe love or peace. But the truth is the message that Jesus preached the most was about the Kingdom of Heaven and that it was near. We aren't really used to the term kingdom anymore because, for the most part, our westernised countries are not ruled by a king with a kingdom. We live within a democracy with a president or a prime minister. In Jesus' day there was a kingdom and that kingdom was Rome. Rome was the world superpower and it was ruled by an emperor called Caesar. It was a kingdom that used its power to suppress the helpless and champion the wealthy. If you lived in the upper-class of this kingdom your goal was to eat, drink and be merry, which was just a superficial shallow life that led to more consumerism and more emptiness. Sound familiar?

Jesus came along and spoke of a different Kingdom with a new king, Himself. And we have been called to share the good news of this new kingdom or the good news of the gospel. The greek word for gospel is *'euangelion'*, it might surprise you to know that the word gospel was used often in the ancient world. For instance, when an emperor of Rome had defeated a great enemy, they couldn't publicise it on a local tv network, or instagram feed, so they would send messengers out to share the *'euangelion'* or the 'good news' of the emperor's great victory. This is what we have been called to do in the world, to share the good news of the gospel and to expand the kingdom around the world.

## What is this new kingdom all about?

Paul the apostle wrote to the church in Rome in Romans 14:17:

> *"For the kingdom of God is not a matter of eating and drinking, but of righteousness, peace and joy in the Holy Spirit."*

Paul says that this new kingdom, the kingdom of God, isn't about surface level superficial things that ultimately fail to fulfil and satisfy. When you break down the word kingdom it is composed of two words: 'Kings - domain'. The kingdom of God Paul is talking about is not a physical kingdom, but a condition. When we pray 'Your kingdom come' we are praying for the condition of heaven to be the conditions here on earth. In a similar vein, New Testament scholar N.T. Wright says:

> *"Jesus's resurrection is the beginning of God's new project not to snatch people away from earth*

> *to heaven but to colonise earth with the life of heaven. That, after all, is what the Lord's Prayer is about."*

When the Apostle Paul wrote about the kingdom of heaven he gives attention to three conditions of the kingdom:

## Righteousness

God came to make humanity righteous. To make you presentable, pleasing and without shame. The message of the kingdom is not to make yourself righteous, then come to God but to bring your broken, sinful, shame-filled self to God because he loves you and wants to make you righteous. This is largely what evangelism is all about. It is about declaring the *'euangelion'* or the good news that Jesus came to make you pleasing, presentable and without shame, all we need to do is put our faith and trust in Jesus.

## Peace

The peace Paul talks about is not the absence of problems. He is speaking about an inner peace that has the ability to withstand the storms of life. The word used for peace in this scripture is the Greek word *'eirene'*, which can convey the sense of an inner rest, well being and harmony. It means to bring together that which had been separated. This of course speaks to our separation from God, but also to bringing together the brokenness within us and around us.

## Joy

The Greek word for joy is *'chara'*, which describes a feeling of inner gladness, delight or rejoicing. Joy in the New Testament is virtually always used to signify a feeling of "happiness" that is based on spiritual realities (and independent of what "happens"). This is what the Holy Spirit produces in you as trust in Him. Paul is saying that this is what the king's-domain is all about, this is the condition we have been invited to live in and we have been called to invite others into this kingdom too.

In just about every foreign country, you will find an embassy of the country you came from. Although that embassy is in a different country, as soon as you walk across the gate of that embassy you are no longer in a foreign country, you are in your home country. It is sometimes referred to as sovereign soil. All the rules or authority of your country apply within that embassy, even though the rule and authority outside of that country are contrastingly different. In a very similar way, as Jesus followers, we have been asked to establish 'Kingdom Embassies' all around our city. Your home is meant to be an embassy, your workplace is meant to be an embassy, your school. As Jesus followers we are called to expand the kingdom of heaven here on earth. We are called to push back the kingdom of darkness and increase the kingdom of heaven.

On top of that, Jesus' message was that the kingdom of Heaven is not far off, not distant, not just one day, but HERE and NOW and all humanity is invited to enter into it. How? Through accepting Jesus, or through Salvation. Our job as Christians is to tell people about the kingdom, to share this good news of the gospel, that everyone is welcome into this new kingdom through Jesus.

## PAUSE AND REFLECT:

- ❖ How does your new understanding of the kingdom change your everyday life?
- ❖ Sometimes the idea of sharing your faith can be daunting. The reason why is because we think it is our job to make people believe. But it is not our job, our job is to simply share what Jesus has done in us, to share why we believe. Never underestimate the power of your testimony.
- ❖ Take some time to write out your testimony. What was your life like before Jesus, how did you come to trust in Jesus and what has He been doing in you since that decision? This is a great way to frame your testimony.
- ❖ Pray and ask God to give you an opportunity and the courage to share your testimony.

## A PRAYER:

*"Father, I thank you for inviting me into your kingdom, I thank you for making me righteous, for giving me your peace and your joy. Give me the courage and the opportunity to share my testimony with others. I want to be a part of expanding your kingdom. Amen."*

# CHAPTER 13

# CONTINUING: PRAY FOR THE SICK

> *"I tell you the truth, anyone who believes in me will do **the same works I have done**, and **even greater works**, because I am going to be with the Father. 13 You can ask for anything in my name, and I will do it, so that the Son can bring glory to the Father. 14 Yes, ask me for anything in my name, and I will do it! (John 14:12-17)*

> *"Jesus sent out the twelve apostles with these instructions... ⁷ Go and announce to them that the **Kingdom of Heaven** is near. **Heal the sick**, raise the dead, cure those with leprosy, and **cast out demons**. Give as freely as you have received! (Matthew 10:5-8)*

I once posted a short statement on my instagram that read *"God is not a reluctant healer, so don't be a reluctant asker."*

Responses of agreement quickly filled the comments section of my instagram, but one comment in particular caught my attention. A friend of mine who I love and respect, responded:

> "So what would it mean if someone enthusiastically asked God for healing, but didn't receive it? Does that mean they weren't audacious enough in their request? Or was God unwilling to help or heal?"

My friend didn't write this because he disagreed with my statement or wanted to be argumentative. He knew there was a lot more nuance and depth to the topic of healing than the statement allowed for. I sat on it for while before I responded with:

> "Great question..There is definitely a great mystery around healing. Here is what I do believe. God is a healer. Sometimes people are healed and sometimes they aren't. I believe that we should pray for healing for ourselves and others and believe God can heal, and that we should be in the habit of doing so. In the same way a parent sometimes gives their kids what they want and sometimes they don't give their kids what they want, it's not because they don't love them, it's because they have other reasons which at the time are unknown to the child. God will one day reveal all, but until then He asked us to keep asking, so I believe our default position should be to ask and believe He can heal."

# CONTINUING: PRAY FOR THE SICK

Jesus was constantly healing people. Every town He went to, He would heal people. He showed His disciples how to heal the sick, then He sent out his disciples to do exactly the same thing (Luke 10:9). I, and many others, believe that Jesus' message to go out and pray for the sick still stands today. But this can be a daunting exercise. *What if I pray and nothing happens? I will look like a fool.* To which I would say - What if something does happen? What if you pray for someone and they do get healed and God gets glorified through your simple act of obedience?

A few truths about healing:

**We are not the healer, but in most cases God uses us as the vehicle for His healing power to flow through.**

It's very important for us to recognise that we are not the healer. God is the healer. Sometimes in scripture we see God healing people without any human agency, but for the most part He uses people as a means to operate His healing power through. You could be a person who God wants to operate His healing power through. What an incredible privilege, if only we would be open to those moments.

**When we pray sometimes people get healed and sometimes they don't. Our responsibility is to step out in faith and pray for the sick.**

I don't know why some people don't get healed and some people do. This is a mystery that one day in heaven I'm sure will be made clear to us. However this should not be a hindrance to praying for others, or lessen our trust or faith in God.

**Jesus, the disciples, and the new testament church prayed for the sick and so should we.**

I encourage you to read the book of Acts. Look how the early followers of Jesus went into different towns preaching the gospel and laying hands on the sick and God's healing power moved through them. In the early church, if anyone was sick they were encouraged to go to the elders or leaders of the church to receive prayer for healing (James 5:14). As disciples and followers of Jesus we should step out in faith and believe that God can heal.

If we are honest most charismatic churches have become closet cessationists. We have given more attention to preaching good ideas and creating engaging services, while ignoring the power that accompanies the gospel. We must never forget that the church is meant to be a space where people engage with the life changing power not just of the word Of God, but the spirit of God.

### How do we pray for the sick?

### 1. Keep in daily connection with God

In order to operate God's healing power it's important to stay connected to the source of that power. The more you spend time with God, the more you will be emboldened with His spirit. His presence will empower you to go and pray for those who are sick.

## 2. Grow in faith

Faith in its simplest definition means to trust or to be convinced by God. The more you get to know God, His character and His power, the more faith or trust you will have in Him. Faith is like a fire. You need to feed it and the more you feed it, the bolder you will become in faith for the healing of others. Faith grows through God's word, prayer, worship and community with others. Faith will also trust that even if God doesn't heal in that situation, He is still good and that God's healing power will have its way in the end (Revelation 21:4).

Faith is a gift from God. You can ask for more. There is an amazing account of a man who asks Jesus to heal his son, but he has an element of doubt. He says to Jesus, "help me with my unbelief" (Mark 9:24). In other words, "Jesus help me to trust that you can heal". We can do the same. If you are struggling to believe Jesus can heal, simply pray *"Jesus help me with my unbelief"*.

## 3. Be bold and be obedient to God's prompting to pray for others.

During Jesus' earthly ministry He would never hesitate to pray for those who were sick or suffering. He would be led by His Father's prompting to go and heal (John 5:19). Here are two simple things you should aim to do every day in order to be ready to pray for people's healing:

- Every morning before you go about your day, tell God that if there is anyone you want me to pray for today, reveal that person to me.

- When someone around you says that they are unwell or struggling with pain of any sort, offer to pray for them.

The more you step out of your comfort zone, the more confident you will become in these moments.

**4. Pray a simple prayer of healing.**

Prayer for healing doesn't need to be elongated or wordy, just make it simple, like Jesus did. When Jesus prayed for people He barely said anything:

> *"Stretch out your hand"* - Matthew 12:13

> *"Get up, pick up your mat and walk"* - John 5:8

> *"Lazarus come forth"* - John 11:43

Jesus prayed simple prayers of healing. Jesus never prayed from a position of begging or pleading, He prayed from a position of authority. When it come to praying for people here is an easy prayer to pray:

> "God, you love (insert name), I declare healing in (insert area of sickness or pain) in Jesus' name. Amen."

## PAUSE AND REFLECT:

- ❖ Take a moment and carefully look through the book of Acts. Note every time God used His followers to bring healing into people's lives.
- ❖ How would you feel if someone you prayed for got healed?
- ❖ Who in your world needs healing that you can pray for right now? Take time to pray for them and look for a moment to pray for them personally.

## A PRAYER:

*"Father, you can do all things. Help me with my unbelief. I want to step out in faith, lay hands on the sick and believe they will recover. Give me courage to step out in faith and pray for those who are sick. Amen."*

# CHAPTER 14

## CONTINUING: Dealing with the Demonic

*"Look, I have given you authority over all the power of the enemy.." Luke 10:19*

Eighteenth century french poet, Charles Baudelaire said:

*"The greatest trick the Devil ever pulled was convincing the world he didn't exist"*

Unfortunately we live in a world that would rather explain away the demonic than confront it. But all throughout Jesus' ministry, He opposed and pushed back the demonic forces in this world. Because of Jesus, the demonic is not meant to be feared but it also should not be ignored. There is an enemy we fight against and we must be ready to push back against his destructive plans.

# CONTINUING: DEALING WITH THE DEMONIC

## Why would we experience demonic opposition?

Once you were a slave to sin (Romans 6:20), and a slave is very little threat to their captors, but when you said yes to putting your hope and trust in Jesus, Colossians 1:13 says:

> *"For He has rescued us from the dominion of darkness and brought us into the kingdom of the Son He loves."*

You are now on God's side, a part of God's kingdom, and are now a part of God's war against the dominion of darkness. Believers having nothing to fear. In fact, a believer who knows who they are in Jesus and is aware of the power of the spirit within them is feared by the enemy.

We must also remember that not everything is spiritual, sometimes it's just a flat tire, or random coincidence or the result of poor decisions. But not everything is natural, sometimes there is a demonic force going against your marriage, your kids, your business, your relationships.

## Spiritual warfare and our part to play as Jesus disciples

There are wars happening right now in different parts of the world, and wars have always been a part of human history. Wars are usually based on two things:

- An Empire or Country looking to expand its territory by overpowering another.
- And those fighting back in order to protect that country or other empires or countries joining in support of that country to fight with them against their enemy.

This same dynamic is happening in the Spiritual realm. There is Satan or in Hebrew śāṭān, which is a title that means 'accuser' or 'adversary', and his demons, and there is God and His angels. They are at war with each other. Satan's plans are to steal, kill and destroy, while God's plans are to rescue, redeem and give abundance of life. The good news is the war has been won, but there are still some battles to be fought.

I know that can sound confusing, but World War II is a great way to illustrate my point. On September 1st, 1939 Nazi Germany invaded Poland and in honouring their guarantee with Poland, Britain and France came to their aid, which was the starting point of the war. The war went on for another six years and ended on May 9th, 1945, but many World War II historians say the war was won on D-day, June 6th, 1944, when 150,000 allied troops landed on the beaches of Normandy in France, pushing back the Nazi army. It was the beginning of the inevitable end for Germany's plan of domination and control. The war was won twelve months before, but there were still battles to be fought.

In the same way when Jesus came and died on the cross, sin, hell and death lost its power. Heaven's invasion of the devil's plan here on earth had begun, the victory of the cross is once and for all. The day will come when victory is complete, but until then we join the kingdom in spiritual warfare as we now push back the kingdom of darkness. Jesus said that His disciples are joining Him in casting out demons and setting the captives free.

## So how do we deal with the demonic?

Paul the apostle in Ephesians 6:10-13 says:

> "A final word: Be strong in the Lord and in his mighty power. 11 Put on all of God's armour so that you will be able to stand firm against all strategies of the devil. 12 For we are not fighting against flesh-and-blood enemies, but against evil rulers and authorities of the unseen world, against mighty powers in this dark world, and against evil spirits in the heavenly places.13 Therefore, put on every piece of God's armour so you will be able to resist the enemy in the time of evil. Then after the battle you will still be standing firm."

## We must recognise the power we have in God.

When you said yes to Jesus, you partnered with God in advancing His kingdom and pushing back the kingdom of darkness. Not only that, you now have God's power backing you as you do it. We are not to be strong in ourselves, but strong in the Lord.

Picture a person standing in front of an ant, there is no match. So it is with God against the devil. The devil and his demons tremble in the presence of God.

## Put on the full armour of God.

Although we belong to God, we are not God, so we must put on the armour of God as listed in Ephesians 6. This is not literal armour but a spiritual one. All of it designed to protect your mind, emotions and your spirit. What is amazing, is that after the Apostle Paul encourages us to put on the armour of God, the next move is to just stand. As if to say the armour does all the fighting on your behalf.

## Use God's word as your weapon.

When Jesus was tempted by Satan, He didn't reply with an aggressive argument. He simply responded with God's word. When you are facing demonic resistance, don't fight back with your words, fight back with God's word. God's word is like a sword in the hands of the believer. Hebrews 4:12 says:

> *"For the word of God is living and active, sharper than any two-edged sword, piercing to the division of soul and of spirit.."*

## Know your authority in Christ.

If you were to step out onto a busy main road and try to stop traffic, it would be extremely difficult, if not impossible. But if you were to step out onto that same road wearing a police uniform, you would be successful. The difference; *authority*. A police officer is a person just like you and me, but has been given authority greater than themselves. Jesus gave authority to His followers so they could come against the demonic. Dr Luke writes down the words of Jesus to His apostles but also to us in Luke 10:19:

> *"Look, I have given you authority over all the power of the enemy..."*

In following Jesus we don't fear the demonic, we confront it. To be a disciple is not so much to fight for victory but from victory.

## PAUSE AND REFLECT:

- ❖ What did you see Jesus doing when He interacted with the demonic?
- ❖ Do you feel confident in confronting the demonic? If not, why not?
- ❖ What scriptures would you use to confront the demonic?

## A PRAYER:

*"Father, I thank you that you rescued me from the kingdom of darkness. I stand upon the fact that I am now strong in the Lord and the power of your might. Help me to grow in courage as I join with you in pushing back the kingdom of darkness. You did not give me a spirit of fear or timidity, but a spirit of power, love and sound mind. Today I pray against any demonic force in my area or my city. I take up the authority you have given me. Amen*

# CHAPTER 15

## CONTINUING: Serve the Poor

> *"If someone has enough money to live well and sees a brother or sister in need but shows no compassion—how can God's love be in that person?18 Dear children, let's not merely say that we love each other; let us show the truth by our actions."*
> (1 John 3:17-18)

It doesn't matter how advanced, free, wealthy or progressive our world gets, there is still so much poverty. There are many reasons why poverty still remains, and we must do our best to fight greed and injustice, but the bigger focus for the Christian is 'what will we do to serve those who are less fortunate?'

The early church lived in a time when there was very clear distinction between the societal classes. There were the really rich and the really poor, and before christianity there was no such thing as social welfare or government aid, especially for people you had nothing to do with. It was the Christian community that invented homeless shelters, hospitals, and movements like social justice. Christianity has always been at the forefront of helping those who are poor or underprivileged.

When you look at the New Testament letters and the early church history you will see how they actively and intentionally served those less fortunate both inside and outside the church.

## Sharing of Resources

One of the most distinctive features of the early church was its practice of communal sharing. Believers would voluntarily pool their resources and possessions to ensure that no one among them was in need. This way of life is described in Acts 2:44-45 and Acts 4:32-35, where it is mentioned that:

> *"All the believers were together and had everything in common... they sold property and possessions to give to anyone who had need."*

## Charitable Giving

The early church encouraged its members to give generously to support those in need. The Apostle Paul, in his letters to a variety of new testament Christian communities, often emphasised the importance of giving to the poor and supporting the work of the ministry. For example, in 2 Corinthians 9:6-8, Paul encourages cheerful and generous giving:

> *"God loves a cheerful giver."*

Charity wasn't just an action, it was an attitude the church had in giving toward those in need.

## Support for Widows and Orphans

Caring for widows and orphans was a significant aspect of early Christian charity. In the book of Acts, the apostles appointed individuals to oversee the distribution of food to widows in need (Acts 6:1-7). James 1:27 emphasises the importance of pure religion as visiting orphans and widows in their distress. I once heard a story about the small village of Yang Jia in China, where 53 families had fostered 166 children, and the majority of the children had complex special needs. One foreign pastor who visited described Yang Jia as a city on a hill, not a village on a mountain. He had seen the effect it had like a lamp on a stand that shows the glory of God to the watching nations. To help widows and orphans is the purest form of the Christian faith because it is a practical example of *'agape'*, God's one way sacrificial love.

## Hospitality

Early Christians were known for their hospitality towards strangers and travellers. This was an extension of the belief in welcoming and caring for others as if they were Christ Himself. The concept of showing kindness to strangers is echoed in Hebrews 13:2:

> *"Do not forget to show hospitality to strangers, for by doing so some people have shown hospitality to angels without knowing it."*

Hospitality for Jesus followers wasn't optional, it was optimal for sharing the love of God. Writer and theologian Henri Nouwen said:

> *"Hospitality means primarily the creation of free space where the stranger can enter and become a friend instead of an enemy. Hospitality is not to change people, but to offer them space where change can take place."*

Opening up homes and the practice of hospitality were the main vehicles for the early church to practically show the love and kindness of God to others. In a world where a person's home is their castle, Jesus leads His followers to take down the walls and turn our homes into havens of loving hospitality.

## Almsgiving

The term "almsgiving" refers to the act of giving to the poor or providing financial assistance. Early Christians were encouraged to practise almsgiving as a way to demonstrate their love for God and their fellow human beings. Jesus taught about the importance of giving to the poor in Matthew 6:2-3:

> *"So when you give to the needy, do not announce it with trumpets, as the hypocrites do in the synagogues and on the streets, to be honoured by others. Truly I tell you, they have received their reward in full. But when you give to the needy, do not let your left hand know what your right hand is doing.."*

There are plenty of generous people in the world who are not Jesus followers, but the difference for Christians is that we are called not to showcase our generosity to the world. We don't do it to receive praise or accolades, we do it because that is simply what Jesus followers do.

## Caring for the Sick

The early church also engaged in caring for the sick. During times of plagues and illnesses, Christians would often provide care and support to the sick, even at the risk of their own lives. This compassionate care for the sick was radical in the ancient world. Where the sick were rejected and ostracised by society, the Christians would be there to care and nurse people back to health. Practically, this looks like taking meals to a sick neighbour, or meal trains to that lady who just got that heartbreaking cancer diagnosis. It also means coming alongside the sick and praying for them.

Practically meeting the needs of the poor or less fortunate is taking God's love and putting it into action.

John Wesley, the founder of the Methodist church and the inspiration behind a welfare initiative called 'Wesley Mission', said:

> *"Do all the good you can, by all the means you can, in all the ways you can, in all the places you can, at all the times you can, to all the people you can, as long as ever you can."*

Remember, the poor are not just those who are homeless and living on the streets, although that is an amazing place to start. It is also the single mum who you know is going through a rough time, or the school kid who doesn't have enough money to go to school camp with his friends, or the university student struggling to pay his school fees and is living on two minute noodles. All these are moments to serve those less fortunate.

The greatest act of love is doing something for someone who you know can do nothing in return. It's one way love. It's Godly love.

## **PAUSE AND REFLECT**

- ❖ Why do you think God cares so much about the poor?
- ❖ It doesn't matter where you live, poverty in its various forms is all around us. Consider how you can practically meet the needs of those around you. A great practice is to put $40 aside, pray at the beginning of the day for God to show you who you can bless and help with that money, whether it be buying food or warm clothing for someone you see in need. The assigned money gives you focused intention, and the prayer will give you focused attention. Try it and watch how God moves through you.

## **A PRAYER:**

"Father, give me the eyes to see and heart to feel for those who are poor and are struggling around me. I want to be your hands and feet in my community. Show me where I can meet the needs in my world. Let my actions be a demonstration of your love for the world. Amen."

# COMMISSIONING PRELUDE

We have covered a lot of ground in this book, and each one of the topics, from foundation to formation, and continuing are not meant to be seen as a checklist that you have now completed. Instead, they represent a new reality and lifestyle you are committing to follow. My hope is that this book acts as a guide you can constantly come back to, helping you as you follow Jesus.

However, this book wasn't just written for you; it was also written for others – your friends, family, or even strangers that God places on your path. You can use it to help them become disciples, just like you. The last chapter of this book is short and simple, yet it points to the final command or commission that Jesus gave us: to go and make disciples. In simple terms, disciples make disciples, and that is what Jesus has asked us to do.

CHAPTER 16

# HELP OTHERS TO BECOME DISCIPLES

The great commission in Matthew 28, was not a suggestion or an option, but a command. We all have many great gifts and callings on our lives, but there is one thing Jesus required all of His followers to do. Once you have become a disciple you now need to help others become a disciple as well. Remember the word disciple means 'apprentice'. To follow Jesus is to commit to a lifelong journey of apprenticeship, and just like an apprenticeship the longer you do it, the more competent and skilled you become. As you grow in this apprenticeship, Jesus now asks you to help others become an apprentice. In fact, Matthew 28 basically says that to be a disciple you need to be making disciples.

So how do you make disciples? A few things you need to know:

# AN INVITATION TO FOLLOW

## Discipleship is not a program, it's a personal journey someone takes with another person

Jesus didn't teach his disciples a program, He showed and taught them a lifestyle to follow. Programs run for a matter of weeks or months, but a lifestyle is a long term commitment. In his book "The Lost Art of Disciple Making", LeRoy Eims brilliantly captures the heart behind helping others become disciples:

> *"Disciples cannot be mass produced, we cannot drop people into a "program" and see disciples emerge at the end of the production line. It takes time to make disciples. It takes individual, personal attention. It takes hours of prayer for them. It takes patience and understanding to teach them how to get into the Word of God for themselves, how to feed and nourish their souls, and by the power of the Holy Spirit how to apply the word to their lives. And it takes being an example to them of all of the above."*

When you help someone to become a disciple, you are committing to a relationship, a journey. This is why many Christians and churches aren't really effective in making disciples because there are no shortcuts to discipleship, only the long road. Helping someone become a disciple is committing to a journey with that person and helping them to follow Jesus.

## Discipleship is largely conversational

We have grown up in classrooms where we sit, listen and take notes. That has been our primary avenue for education and learning, but to be a disciple in Jesus' day was to converse, to bring up a topic and talk about it back and forth, to wrestle out complex or difficult topics, to allow for questions. This is still the best way to help someone become a disciple. Teach them, but don't make it a one way conversation. Ask them questions about the topic and allow them to ask questions as well. Conversation takes sharing our thoughts and feelings, it takes engagement of our minds and it brings closeness between people. Discipleship should never be seen as a lecture hall, but a round table where everyone is invited to contribute.

## Discipleship is not about following a set of rules, it's about helping others follow a person

Rules are great, they keep much of our society safe and in order. In fact the bible is also full of "rules" and all of them are designed to help us live a more abundant life. But rules are not relational. If rules were enough, then God could have stopped with the ten commandments. But God is not a God of rules alone, He is firstly a God of relationship. If you have a relationship then the rules are seen as acts of love, and not a demanding requirement. As a child grows and experiences the love of a parent, the child knows that, in love, the parent will tell the child what is wrong or dangerous, and it's from the foundation of love that the child trusts the parents' rules. Jesus came and put on flesh so that we could have a relationship with Him and have a loving example to follow. Rules alone lead to legalism, which never produces loving acts of obedience.

In helping someone become a disciple, it's extremely important that we help them realise this is not about following rules, but following closely to the loving example of Jesus. When Jesus said "Teach them to obey all I have commanded you" it was obedience built on the reality of infinitely loving God. It's so much easier to obey God, when you know how much he loves you and wants what is best for you.

You don't have to wait to be a perfect disciple before you help someone become a disciple.

#### How can I practically equip someone to become a disciple?

There is no one size fits all when it comes to discipleship, however there are key ingredients we see from Jesus and the early church's example. What are those ingredients? Everything we have just covered. If you want to equip someone to become a disciple all you need to do is take someone through exactly what you have just learnt:

- Connection
    - The Father Heart of God
    - The Work of the Cross
    - The person and power of the Holy Spirit
    - Community accountability
    - Reflective reading

# HELP OTHERS TO BECOME DISCIPLES

  - Persistent prayer
  - Total stewardship
  - Sabbath
- Continuing
  - Pray for the sick
  - Dealing with the demonic
  - Expand the Kingdom
  - Serve the poor
- Commissioning
  - Help others to become a disciple.

## How long will this take?

There is no set time frame, but remember this isn't a program, it's just a means to help equip others to become a disciple. At the end of covering the topics in this book, people won't become perfect disciples of Jesus, but you will have equipped them with all the tools they need to follow. It's not about perfection, it's about progress. But Jesus gave us the responsibility to help others progress in their journey to follow him. In the words of Timothy Keller:

> *"Discipleship is not a sprint; it's a marathon. It's a lifelong journey of following Jesus and becoming more like him each day."*

I want to encourage you to take the time to help someone else become a disciple. To passionately and patiently walk someone through this content. Jesus gave all those who follow him this commission. Go and make disciples of all nations. For thousands of years many have done exactly that, impacting billions of people throughout history…now it's your turn. It's time to go!

## PAUSE AND REFLECT:

- ❖ Many people feel like they are not good enough or qualified enough to help someone become a disciple. Take time to read through the gospels and consider the qualifications and character of the disciples.
- ❖ Think about who has helped you on your discipleship journey. What did they do that made an impact on your faith journey?
- ❖ Who could you help on their journey of discipleship?

## A PRAYER:

*"Father, I want to become a greater disciple of you and help others to become a disciple as well. I thank you that you gave me your word, your example and the person of the Holy Spirit to help me on this journey. Help me to help others as they follow you into discipleship. Amen."*

# EPILOGUE

2020 and 2021 were two of the craziest years in recent history. It felt like being in a car accident – we were driving along, just on our journey, and out of nowhere, we were t-boned by a worldwide pandemic. We spun out of control, with no sense of direction, and finally crashed into a whole new reality that would reshape our lives. We all walked away dazed and disoriented. But in the midst of the chaos, I believe God was working. God used the pandemic to reveal that our attention and focus had strayed from His original plan. We had celebrated church attendance and had unknowingly drifted into cultural Christianity. We had neglected spiritual maturity and the commission to make disciples.

Jesus never asked us to grow the church; He asked us to make disciples. What's the difference? FOCUS.

If our focus is on growing the church, we will be content with a crowd. But if our focus is on discipleship, our joy will come from people coming to Jesus and then following Him into spiritual maturity. As much as we may want to forget the pandemic, we must never forget the lessons it taught us. Sunday-centric Christianity cannot withstand the storms of life, but disciples can.

Being a disciple is not an easy journey; Jesus said in Matthew 16:24:

> *"Then Jesus said to His disciples, 'Whoever wants to be My disciple must deny themselves and take up their cross and follow Me.'"*

The journey of discipleship begins and continues with self-denial and carrying a cross – two concepts that radically oppose our myopic consumerist culture.

Self-denial doesn't mean your personality and uniqueness disappear. What Jesus is saying is that your old way of forming an identity, of seeking a sense of self, must come to an end. You have to let it die, and in return, He will give you a completely new identity. You will discover your true self. As Timothy Keller puts it:

> *"Discipleship isn't just about aligning your will with Jesus'; it's about reshaping your heart entirely. A disciple isn't merely someone who sets new priorities; a disciple finds a new identity."*

The cross is also a significant part of this journey. In the Roman Empire, a cross symbolised humiliation, despair, and defeat. However, in the Kingdom of God, a Cross signifies victory over our destructive sinful desires and the power to live a new life filled with love and fulfilment. When Jesus said, "Take up your cross," He meant for us to lay down our agenda and embrace His.

The invitation to the discipleship journey was rejected by many because they couldn't see past the demands of self-denial and carrying a cross. Yet, if you were to ask those who responded to the call to follow, to deny self, to bear a cross, they would all joyfully answer that what seemed like losing life was, in fact, discovering fulfilment. What appeared to be death was, in reality, life – and life more abundant. Or, in the words of the late Brennan Manning:

> *"Following Jesus means living a life of radical love, profound peace, and unshakable joy."*

Becoming a disciple of Jesus is an invitation to follow closely. I hope you will respond to that call and join the ranks of countless others throughout history who have truly followed Jesus.

# ACKNOWLEDGMENTS

It has been a joy putting together this book, but it would not have been possible without the help of many. I want to express my gratitude to Kyleen Lopez, who edited this book – you are absolutely brilliant. I also want to extend my thanks to Matt Danswan and Ark House Publishing; you have always been so helpful and easy to work with. I'd like to acknowledge my sister, Lee, who has been a massive help with both my book cover and our website. Additionally, I want to appreciate the amazing Brittany Vandestraat, who designed the cool icon featured on the cover. One small image says so much – you're amazing. I want to express my gratitude to those who have invested in my life and consistently pointed me towards Jesus. And last but not least, I want to thank my wife, Alanna, and my kids, who freed me up to be able to complete this book.

Printed in the USA
CPSIA information can be obtained
at www.ICGtesting.com
LVHW011529070124
768352LV00047B/1054